Diet recommendations during breast cancer

Diet can support the affected organs and is not a treatment for the disease. Please check these recommendations always with a nutrition consultant, therapist, doctor or dietician. The recipes and the list of ingredients are supporting the conventional medical therapy.
The calorie disclosures of fresh ingredients (fruit and vegetables) vary according to quality and time of harvest. The contents were checked by a dietician and a nutrition consultant for the Traditional Chinese Medicine (TCM).

Author:
©2017 Josef Miligui
www.ebns.at

AF206454

Source:
The lists are created from the EBNS database for nutritional counseling. The database is used by dietitians, therapists and doctors for advising the patient / client.

Literature:
The specialist literature and the training documents of the German and Austrian dietary and traditional Chinese medicine serve as a knowledge base. We have used the documents as a basis of knowledge, adapted it to our experience and completed them.
http://di-book.com

Title Photo:
©2008 Erika Weixlbaumer

Production and publishing:
BoD – Books on Demand, Norderstedt
ISBN: 9783746098036

Diet recommendations during breast cancer

1 Treatment strategy..5
2 Avoid 5
3 Breakfast kkal. per serving 6
4 Snack 7
5 Lunch 7
6 Afternoon...8
7 Dinner...9
8 Any time 10
9 Recipes 11
   9.1   Andalusian fish pot..11
   9.2   Antipasti..12
   9.3   Apple - banana cream 12
   9.4   Avocado with lemon 13
   9.5   Barley soup...14
   9.6   Basic recipe for a chicken broth worming.............14
   9.7   Basic recipe for a fish broth 15
   9.8   Basic recipe for a vegetable soup, nutritious.......16
   9.9   Basmati rice + Zucchini tofu dish 17
   9.10   Bean paste piquant sweet....................................17
   9.11   Beluga lentil stew with vegetables.......................18
   9.12   Bilberry - curd cheese with Acai powder..............19
   9.13   Breakfast - Rice with fruits 20
   9.14   Breakfast with cheese..20
   9.15   Broccoli and Parmesan spread on toast bread 21
   9.16   Broccoli cream soup 22
   9.17   Bulgur with tomatoes and fresh herbs 22
   9.18   Carrot drink...23
   9.19   Carrot Risotto 24
   9.20   Cod soup with tomatoes 24
   9.21   Colorful rice dish...25
   9.22   Compote from blueberries.....................................26
   9.23   Cottage cheese with steamed fruit 27
   9.24   Couscous Salad 27
   9.25   Cranberry juice 28
   9.26   Curry rice with raisins and nuts 28
   9.27   Delicately spiced zucchini with tomatoes.............29
   9.28   Fast polenta with avocado and spring onion.........30
   9.29   Fennel and potato gratin.......................................31
   9.30   Fennel with roasted walnuts.................................32

9.31	Fennel-Rice Soup	32
9.32	Fine Russian borscht	33
9.33	Fish soup with white wine, laurel and marjoram	34
9.34	Fried apple	35
9.35	Fruit juice	35
9.36	Grilled salmon steaks with cauliflower and potatoes	36
9.37	Grilled tomatoes with cheese filling	37
9.38	Halibut with tomato and garlic sauce	38
9.39	Indian Dal soup	39
9.40	Japanese algae soup	40
9.41	Kohlrabi in chervil sauce with potatoes	40
9.42	Lasagne with tofu cream	41
9.43	Leek and potato gratin	42
9.44	Lentil and chestnut soup with curry	43
9.45	Lettuce with fresh cheese	43
9.46	Melanzani with olive oil and turmeric	44
9.47	Milk rice vanilla - with cherries	45
9.48	Millet with shiitake mushrooms and avocado	45
9.49	Miso soup with tofu	46
9.50	Muesli with Acai Powder	47
9.51	Noodles with vegetable and tomato sauce	47
9.52	Oat flakes with aromatic spices	48
9.53	Oatmeal soup with spring onion and carrots	49
9.54	Pear juice	49
9.55	Pear with candy sugar and sticky rice	50
9.56	Potato cream with herbs and fresh cheese	50
9.57	Potato-basil soup	51
9.58	Puréed banana	52
9.59	Quick flakes with compote or jam	52
9.60	Quick zucchini soup	53
9.61	Radish, apple and yogurt fresh food	54
9.62	Red lentils with avocado and radish	54
9.63	Reissue soup with fresh fruits	55
9.64	Ribbon noodles with leaf spinach	56
9.65	Rice congee with honey pear and black sesame	57
9.66	Rice with stewed vegetables	58
9.67	Roasted barley patties	58
9.68	Roasted nuts	59
9.69	Semolina porridge with banana	60
9.70	Semolina soup with vegetables	60
9.71	Spelled-grid porridge with berries of the season	61
9.72	Spicy avocado cream with cottage cheese	62
9.73	Spicy Tofu Vegetable Pan	63

9.74	Spring salad	63
9.75	Strawberry bananas mash	64
9.76	Supplementary nutrition	65
9.77	Sweet potato pancakes with basil pesto	65
9.78	Sweet rice with apples	66
9.79	Szeged fishbowl	67
9.80	Tea Green tea	67
9.81	Tomato soup	68
9.82	Tsampa	69
9.83	Vegetable bowl with Provencal pistou	69
9.84	Vegetable juice	70
9.85	Vegetable miso soup with tofu	71
9.86	Warming carrot soup	72
9.87	Yellow lentil soup	72
9.88	Zucchini with basil pesto	73
10	Effects of food	75
10.1	Use ingredients: recommendable	75
10.2	Use ingredients: yes	76
10.3	Use ingredients: little	81
10.4	Do not use contra-acting foods	82
11	Herbs and their effects	82
11.1	Basil	82
11.2	Nettles	83
11.3	Dill	83
11.4	Chervil dried	83
11.5	Coriander	83
11.6	Herbs various	83
11.7	Cress	83
11.8	Chives	83
11.9	Lovage	83
11.10	Lily bulbs	84
11.11	Dandelion (young plants)	84
11.12	Marjoram	84
11.13	Oregano dried	84
11.14	Parsley	84
11.15	Peppermint	84
11.16	Rosemary	84
11.17	Sage	84
11.18	Sorrel	85
11.19	Black caraway	85
11.20	Thyme dried	85
11.21	King Solomon's-seal	85
11.22	Yam root, yam root tuber	85

11.23   Lemon Balm (fresh) 85
12 Basics of Nutrition 86
12.1   Nutrition 86
12.2   Recipes 88
12.3   Foodstuffs 88
12.4   Herbs 89
13 Other dietic-books 90

1   Treatment strategy

Fats: olive oil, rapeseed oil, peanut oil and linseed oil.
It is recommended to eat sea fish at least twice a week.
Carrots, cabbage, spinach, corn salad, broccoli, parsley, apricot, honeydew melon, paprika, fennel, horseradish, blackcurrant, kiwi, orange, vegetable oils, nuts, fish, cereals, tomatoes, apples, berries, leeks, grapes, green tea. Especially fruits and vegetables contain these important ingredients.
Antihormonal effects of phytoestrogens and indoles:
Soy (Concentrated soya preparations are not recommended).
Indoles are contained in vegetables: broccoli, cabbage sprouts, carobiola, cabbage, radishes, radish, mustard, horseradish, rocket, cress. (Indoles are very sensitive to heat and are destroyed during a long cooking time).
Rich fiber lowers estrogen levels in the blood. Fruits and vegetables (5 servings per day) plus cereal products, preferably whole wheat.
Drink plenty of water and tea or fruit juices heavily diluted.

2   Avoid

Reduce the consumption of animal fats but also as widely "healthy" propagated oils such as safflower oil, grape seed oil or sunflower oil. These are unfavorable for the mammary gland due to their high omega-6 fatty acid content.

Little alcohol. You should not consume more than 20 g of alcohol per day. This is equivalent to about 1 small beer or 1 - 2 small glasses wine.

3 Breakfast

kkal. per serving

Apple - banana cream 110
Avocado with lemon 289
Breakfast with cheese 593
Broccoli and Parmesan spread on toast bread 148
Bulgur with tomatoes and fresh herbs 205
Carrot drink 143
Carrot Risotto 308
Colorful rice dish 437
Cottage cheese with steamed fruit 214
Couscous Salad 338
Cranberry juice 43
Curry rice with raisins and nuts 275
Fast polenta with avocado and spring onion 449
Fennel-Rice Soup 155
Fried apple 408
Fruit juice 175
Miso soup with tofu 51
Muesli with Acai Powder 391
Noodles with vegetable and tomato sauce 561
Oat flakes with aromatic spices 280
Oatmeal soup with spring onion and carrots 134
Pear juice 180
Potato cream with herbs and fresh cheese 217
Potato-basil soup 95
Puréed banana 144
Quick flakes with compote or jam 189
Radish, apple and yogurt fresh food 77
Reissue soup with fresh fruits 143
Rice congee with honey pear and black sesame 158
Roasted barley patties 398
Roasted nuts 973
Semolina porridge with banana 307
Semolina soup with vegetables 105
Spelled-grid porridge with berries of the season 243
Spicy avocado cream with cottage cheese 613
Spicy Tofu Vegetable Pan 241
Sweet rice with apples 155
Tea Green tea 2
Vegetable miso soup with tofu 106

4 Snack

Apple - banana cream 110
Radish, apple and yogurt fresh food 77
Spelled-grid porridge with berries of the season 243

5 Lunch

Andalusian fish pot 347
Antipasti 100
Avocado with lemon 289
Barley soup 265
Basmati rice + Zucchini tofu dish 145
Bean paste piquant sweet 311
Beluga lentil stew with vegetables 201
Broccoli and Parmesan spread on toast bread 148
Broccoli cream soup 98
Bulgur with tomatoes and fresh herbs 205
Carrot drink 143
Carrot Risotto 308
Cod soup with tomatoes 176
Colorful rice dish 437
Compote from blueberries 49
Cottage cheese with steamed fruit 214
Couscous Salad 338
Cranberry juice 43
Curry rice with raisins and nuts 275
Delicately spiced zucchini with tomatoes 203
Fast polenta with avocado and spring onion 449
Fennel and potato gratin 147
Fennel with roasted walnuts 342
Fennel-Rice Soup 155
Fine Russian borscht 171
Fish soup with white wine, laurel and marjoram 199
Fried apple 408
Fruit juice 175
Grilled salmon steaks with cauliflower and potatoes 329
Grilled tomatoes with cheese filling 469
Halibut with tomato and garlic sauce 319
Indian Dal soup 255
Japanese algae soup 47
Kohlrabi in chervil sauce with potatoes 187
Lasagne with tofu cream 301
Leek and potato gratin 368

Lentil and chestnut soup with curry 176
Lettuce with fresh cheese 802
Melanzani with olive oil and turmeric 432
Millet with shiitake mushrooms and avocado 559
Miso soup with tofu 51
Muesli with Acai Powder 391
Noodles with vegetable and tomato sauce 561
Oatmeal soup with spring onion and carrots 134
Potato cream with herbs and fresh cheese 217
Potato-basil soup 95
Puréed banana 144
Quick zucchini soup 41
Red lentils with avocado and radish 268
Reissue soup with fresh fruits 143
Ribbon noodles with leaf spinach 722
Rice congee with honey pear and black sesame 158
Rice with stewed vegetables 166
Roasted barley patties 398
Roasted nuts 973
Semolina porridge with banana 307
Semolina soup with vegetables 105
Spelled-grid porridge with berries of the season 243
Spicy avocado cream with cottage cheese 613
Spicy Tofu Vegetable Pan 241
Spring salad 162
Sweet potato pancakes with basil pesto 625
Sweet rice with apples 155
Szeged fishbowl 280
Tea Green tea 2
Tomato soup 100
Vegetable bowl with Provencal pistou 137
Vegetable miso soup with tofu 106
Warming carrot soup 133
Yellow lentil soup 155
Zucchini with basil pesto 467

6   Afternoon

Apple - banana cream 110
Fast polenta with avocado and spring onion 449
Pear with candy sugar and sticky rice 217
Radish, apple and yogurt fresh food 77
Spelled-grid porridge with berries of the season 243

7   Dinner

Andalusian fish pot.. 347
Avocado with lemon 289
Barley soup... 265
Basmati rice + Zucchini tofu dish 145
Beluga lentil stew with vegetables 201
Broccoli cream soup.. 98
Carrot drink.. 143
Carrot Risotto.. 308
Cod soup with tomatoes.. 176
Compote from blueberries... 49
Cranberry juice.. 43
Curry rice with raisins and nuts... 275
Delicately spiced zucchini with tomatoes 203
Fennel and potato gratin 147
Fennel with roasted walnuts 342
Fennel-Rice Soup 155
Fine Russian borscht 171
Fish soup with white wine, laurel and marjoram.................... 199
Fried apple... 408
Fruit juice... 175
Grilled salmon steaks with cauliflower and potatoes 329
Grilled tomatoes with cheese filling....................................... 469
Halibut with tomato and garlic sauce 319
Indian Dal soup... 255
Japanese algae soup 47
Kohlrabi in chervil sauce with potatoes 187
Lasagne with tofu cream 301
Leek and potato gratin 368
Lentil and chestnut soup with curry....................................... 176
Melanzani with olive oil and turmeric 432
Miso soup with tofu 51
Pear juice... 180
Pear with candy sugar and sticky rice.................................... 217
Potato-basil soup 95
Quick zucchini soup 41
Red lentils with avocado and radish 268
Reissue soup with fresh fruits.. 143
Rice congee with honey pear and black sesame 158
Rice with stewed vegetables 166
Roasted barley patties 398
Roasted nuts.. 973

Semolina porridge with banana 307
Semolina soup with vegetables 105
Spelled-grid porridge with berries of the season 243
Spicy avocado cream with cottage cheese 613
Spicy Tofu Vegetable Pan.. 241
Sweet potato pancakes with basil pesto 625
Sweet rice with apples.. 155
Tea Green tea.. 2
Tomato soup.. 100
Vegetable bowl with Provencal pistou... 137
Vegetable miso soup with tofu... 106
Warming carrot soup... 133
Yellow lentil soup 155

8 Any time

Avocado with lemon 289
Bilberry - curd cheese with Acai powder 237
Carrot drink... 143
Compote from blueberries.. 49
Cranberry juice... 43
Fruit juice.. 175
Milk rice vanilla - with cherries 394
Miso soup with tofu 51
Muesli with Acai Powder 391
Pear juice... 180
Puréed banana 144
Rice congee with honey pear and black sesame 158
Roasted nuts.. 973
Semolina porridge with banana 307
Semolina soup with vegetables 105
Strawberry bananas mash.. 30
Supplementary nutrition 1045
Tea Green tea... 2

9   Recipes

(recommendable) = You can use more.
(little) = You should use less than specified or omit.

9.1   Andalusian fish pot

Strengthens immune system, prevents cancer, dissolves stagnation, promotes weight loss. Good to fight immunodeficiency, loss of appetite, flatulence, high blood pressure, depressions, diabetes, diarrhea, stimulates appetite.
Cooking time approx. 30 min
Calories p. portion: 348
4 portions
Allergens: ADLO

Quantity of ingredients:
Basic recipe for a vegetable soup (nutritious) 2 cups / 500g. (recommended)
Onion (spring onion) 2 pieces / 40g. (yes)
Olive oil 1 table spoon / 20g. (recommended)
Lemon peel 1/2 piece / 3g. (yes)
Bay leaf 1 piece / 1g. (yes)
Potato 5/8 oz / 200g. (yes)
Cod 3/4 lbs / 300g. (recommended)
White wine 4 table spoons / 80g. (little)
Lemon juice 1/2 teaspoon / 10g. (yes)
Salt 1 pinch / 1g. (little)
Pepper (ground) 1 pinch / 0,2g. (yes)
Parsley 1 table spoon / 15g. (recommended)
White bread (wheat bread) 8 slices / 250g. (little)

Cooking instructions:
Boil the vegetable broth with small spring onion, olive oil, grated lemon peel and bay leaf. Boil covered for 10 minutes. Add the peeled, diced potatoes and boil in about 8 minutes. Add fish pieces and white wine and switch to small heat. In the slightly boiling broth put the fish and boil it a few minutes. Season with lemon juice, salt and pepper. Serve with parsley sprinkled.
White bread as a side dish.

9.2 Antipasti

Improves blood circulation, anti-inflammatory, relieves pain. Diuretic, promotes digestion, reduces blood pressure. antioxidativ, antibacterial, affects anorexia, improves digestion, flatulence, stomach weakness, stimulating.
Cooking time approx. 40 min
Calories p. portion: 100
3 portions
Allergens:

Quantity of ingredients:
Pepperoni 1 piece / 5g. (yes)
Lemon juice 1 table spoon / 10g. (yes)
Aubergine 1 piece / 300g. (yes)
Tomato 4 pieces / 200g. (recommended)
Zucchini 5/8 oz / 200g. (yes)
Lemon peel 1/2 piece / 3g. (yes)
Olive oil 1 table spoon / 15g. (recommended)
Basil (fresh) 8 leaves / 5g. (yes)
Salt 1 pinch / 0,5g. (little)
Coriander 1/2 teaspoon / 2g. (yes)

Cooking instructions:
Preheat the oven to 250 degrees Celsius and bake the hot peppers until the bowl becomes dark (about 20 minutes). Cover the hot peppers with a clear film and allow to cool. Peel the skin and cut into strips about 2 cm wide. Cut tomatoes in half and spread with oil in slices of aubergine and bake in the oven at 200 degrees golden brown (about 10 minutes) Fry the zucchini slices in the grill pan (without fat).
Mix everything together, mix the marinade of olive oil, salt and lemon peel and pour over the vegetables, sprinkle with coriander. Leave for 1 hour.

9.3 Apple - banana cream

Regulates gastrointestinal function, provides vitamin C, cholesterol lowering, reduces inflammation, diuretic, improves blood circulation.
Cooking time approx. 15 min
Calories p. portion: 110
4 portions
Allergens:

Quantity of ingredients:
Apple (sour) 7/8 lbs / 400g. (recommended)
Water 3/4 cup - 6 oz / 200g. (yes)
Orange peel 1/4 piece / 5g. (yes)
Lemon peel 1/2 piece / 2g. (yes)
Sugar brown 2 teaspoons / 6g. (little)
Cinnamon sticks 1 piece / 0g. (yes)
Banana 1 piece / 150g. (recommended)
Acerola fruit nectar or powder 1 teaspoon / 2g. (recommended)
Orange juice 1/2 piece / 50g. (recommended)
Lemon juice 1 table spoon / 10g. (yes)

Cooking instructions:
Cut the apple into fine slices, bring water to boil and add the apple slices, orange- and lemon peel, sugar and cinnamon and simmer about 7 minutes. The apples should be almost soft. Remove acerola and the cinnamon stick. Mix the apple, the banana, the orange juice and the lemon juice.

9.4 Avocado with lemon

Good to fight insomnia, inflammation, swelling, pain and itching. Is calming.
Cooking time approx. 5 min
Calories p. portion: 289
1 portions
Allergens:

Quantity of ingredients:
Avocado 1/2 piece / 120g. (recommended)
Lemon juice 1/2 piece / 10g. (yes)
Salt 1 pinch / 1g. (little)

Cooking instructions:
Halve the avocado, remove the core, add the lemon juice, salt a little and eat with a spoon.

9.5 Barley soup

Diuretic, forcing spleen, supports urination, stimulates liver function, antioxidativ, promotes digestion, detoxifying, reduces blood lipids, stimulates, dissolves stagnation.
Cooking time approx. 25 min
Calories p. portion: 265
2 portions
Allergens: A

Quantity of ingredients:
Barley 1 cup / 120g. (yes)
Salt 1 pinch / 1g. (little)
Ginger fresh 1/2 teaspoon / 1g. (yes)
Olive oil 1 table spoon / 10g. (recommended)
Parsley 2 table spoons / 30g. (recommended)
Water 1 1/2 cups / 240g. (yes)

Cooking instructions:
Roast the barley in the pan, then grind it to the ground, and boil with water, some salt and ginger to a mash. Before serving add oil and parsley.

Variant: You can add a better taste to the dish if you cook it with prepared vegetable or meat broth.

9.6 Basic recipe for a chicken broth worming

Strengthens blood, strengthens bone marrow, reduces blood pressure, strengthens immune system, prevents cancer, reduces radiation damage, promotes sweating, dissolves stagnation, good to fight loss of appetite, flatulence.
Cooking time approx. 2-3 hours
Calories p. portion: 90
9 portions
Allergens: L

Quantity of ingredients:
Chicken meat 1/2 piece / 600g. (little)
Carrot 2 pieces / 150g. (recommended)
Leek 1 stick / 45g. (recommended)
Celery root 1 piece / 500g. (yes)
Ginger fresh 2 slices / 2g. (yes)
Fenugreek (Trigonella foenum-graecum) 1 teaspoon / 2g. (yes)

Juniper berry 1 teaspoon / 3g. (yes)
Bay leaf 3 pieces / 2g. (yes)
Water 4 cup / 900g. (yes)

Cooking instructions:
Remove chicken parts from fat. Place chicken pieces in a saucepan
with hot water and heat till it boils briefly, skimming any resulting foam.
Add coarsely chopped vegetables and all spices and cook over medium
heat for 2 to 3 hours. Strain the finished soup. Throw away vegetables
and bones.
Tip: If you want to use the meat as a soup insert, take out after 45
minutes and return only the bones in the soup.
Refrigerate for later use.

9.7 Basic recipe for a fish broth

Strengthens the kidneys, promotes watering, reduces blood pressure,
strengthens immune system, prevents cancer, reduces radiation
damage. Low in cholesterol and protein rich. Improves blood circulation,
stimulates appetite.
Cooking time approx. 40 min
Calories p. portion: 128
5 portions
Allergens: DLO

Quantity of ingredients:
Fish pieces mixed (fresh water) 3/4 lbs / 300g. (recommended)
Celery root 1/4 lbs - 4oz / 120g. (yes)
Leek 2 inches / 10g. (recommended)
Carrot 2 pieces / 150g. (recommended)
White wine 1/2 cup / 125g. (little)
Lemon 1/2 piece / 50g. (yes)
Bay leaf 2 leaves / 2g. (yes)
Peppercorns 3 pieces / 2g. (yes)
Olive oil 1 table spoon / 10g. (recommended)
Water 2 cup / 450g. (yes)

Cooking instructions:
Fry celery, chopped carrots and leeks in olive oil, add bay leaf and
peppercorns, add pieces of fish and sauté briefly. Add water, add little
white wine or lemon. Simmer gently for 30 minutes. Skim off the
resulting foam several times. In the end, sift the ingredients through a
cloth. Refrigerate for later use

9.8 Basic recipe for a vegetable soup, nutritious

Reduces blood pressure, strengthens immune system, prevents cancer, forcing spleen, dissolves stagnation, promotes weight loss. Good to fight immunodeficiency, high blood pressure, depressions, diabetes, diarrhea, reduces blood lipids.
Cooking time approx. 2-3 hours
Calories p. portion: 48
5 portions
Allergens: L

Quantity of ingredients:
Olive oil 1 table spoon / 4g. (recommended)
Onion white 1 piece / 60g. (yes)
Carrot 3 pieces / 200g. (recommended)
Parsnip 3/8 lbs - 6oz / 150g. (yes)
Celery root 1 cup / 100g. (yes)
Ginger fresh 1/2 teaspoon / 2g. (yes)
Lemon 1/2 piece / 25g. (yes)
Juniper berry 6 pieces / 6g. (yes)
Thyme dried 1 pinch / 1g. (yes)
Lovage 1 table spoon / 3g. (yes)
Bay leaf 2 leaves / 1g. (yes)
Salt 1 pinch / 1g. (little)
Water 3 cups / 650g. (yes)

Cooking instructions:
Cut the vegetables into cubes.
Heat oil in hot pot, fry shortly onions and vegetables.
Add cold water, then add ginger, bay leaf and lemon juice.
Season with juniper, thyme and lovage. Cover for 2 - 3 hours on a low heat and simmer.
The used vegetables should be thrown away.
The basic recipe serves as a soup base and to refine vegetables, legumes or cereals.
If you want to eat vegetable soup immediately, add the desired vegetables half an hour before.
Refrigerate for later use.

9.9 Basmati rice + Zucchini tofu dish

Diuretic, supports urination, harmonizes spleen and stomach, reduces flatulence, good to fight body overweight and high blood pressure. Antioxidativ, promotes digestion, perspiration, reduces blood lipids, forcing spleen.
Cooking time approx. 20 min
Calories p. portion: 146
4 portions
Allergens: E

Quantity of ingredients:
Soy Tofu 5/8 lbs - 8oz / 250g. (recommended)
Olive oil 2 table spoons / 6g. (recommended)
Coriander 1/2 teaspoon / 4g. (yes)
Ginger fresh 1/2 teaspoon / 4g. (yes)
Rice Basmati 1/2 cup / 60g. (yes)
Water 3 cups / 200g. (yes)
Zucchini 1 piece / 700g. (yes)

Cooking instructions:
Cut tofu cubes and marinate with olive oil, tamari, crushed coriander and ginger. Leave at least 1 hour.

Cook Basmati rice with the water. You can season with onion and cardamom.
Roast zucchini and tofu in pan in the hot oil for approx. 5-7 min.
Serve rice and tofu on a plate.
Add the parsley.

Can also be used as a salad for the home and on the go.

9.10 Bean paste piquant sweet

Supports urination, lowers cholesterol, prevents arteriosclerosis, antioxidativ. Promotes digestion, helps to digest fat, supports urination, reduces blood pressure.
Cooking time approx. 1 hour
Calories p. portion: 311
1 portions
Allergens: MO

Quantity of ingredients:
Black beans 1 cup / 120g. (yes)
Ginger fresh 1 inch / 3g. (yes)
Boxhorn clover seeds 1/2 teaspoon / 2g. (yes)
Tomato paste 1 table spoon / 10g. (yes)
Olive oil 2 table spoons / 20g. (recommended)
Pumpkin seed oil 1 dash / 3g. (little)
Mustard 1 knife tip / 1g. (recommended)
Radish horseradish 1 teaspoon (grated) / 2g. (recommended)
Pepper (ground) 1 pinch / 0,5g. (yes)
Garlic 2 cloves / 3g. (recommended)
Salt 1 pinch / 1g. (little)
Sugar molasses 2 table spoons / 20g. (little)
Lemon peel 1/2 piece / 1g. (yes)

Cooking instructions:
Boil beans (with spices and ginger), drain water and puree. Season with spices.

Refine with sugar beet syrup and lemon peel.

9.11 Beluga lentil stew with vegetables

Promotes sweating, dissolves stagnation. Relieves constipation, strengthens mother milk production, stimulates nerves, detoxifying, reduces inflammation, improves blood circulation. Strengthens heart and kidney, diuretic, calms the stomach, promotes digestion.
Cooking time approx. 20 min
Calories p. portion: 201
5 portions
Allergens:

Quantity of ingredients:
Lentils 1 1/2 cups / 240g. (yes)
Water 4-5 cups / 500g. (yes)
Carrot 3 pieces / 150g. (recommended)
Leek 1 piece / 300g. (recommended)
Kohlrabi 1/2 piece / 200g. (recommended)
Tomato 2 pieces / 80g. (recommended)
Onion white 1 piece / 50g. (yes)
Bay leaf 2 leaves / 1g. (yes)
Fennel 1 piece / 250g. (recommended)
Star anise 2 pieces / 1g. (yes)

Juniper berry 6 pieces / 2g. (yes)
Olive oil 2 table spoons / 30g. (recommended)
Salt 1 pinch / 1g. (little)
Ginger fresh 1/2 teaspoon / 2g. (yes)
Black caraway 1 pinch / 1g. (yes)

Cooking instructions:
Heat oil in hot pot. Fry onions and add diced vegetables and spices,
lentils (washed well) and salt. Cover with cold water (3 fingers wide)
and cook for 20 minutes on a low heat.
Sprinkle with fresh herbs and black cumin

Goes well with rice!

9.12 Bilberry - curd cheese with Acai powder

Good to fight weakness, belching, diabetes, acute or chronic
obstruction of the bowel, skin problems. Laxative, antibacterial effect.
Antioxidant.
Cooking time approx. 10 min
Calories p. portion: 238
2 portions
Allergens: GH

Quantity of ingredients:
Blueberry 5/8 oz / 200g. (recommended)
Orange juice 2 table spoons / 10g. (recommended)
Maple syrup 1 table spoon / 5g. (recommended)
Almond 1 table spoon / 5g. (recommended)
Curd cheese 20% 5/8 lbs - 8oz / 250g. (yes)
Sugar cane sugar 1 table spoon / 9g. (little)
Acai powder 2 teaspoons / 5g. (recommended)
Cinnamon ground 1 pinch / 0,5g. (yes)

Cooking instructions:
Rinse the blueberries in a sieve and pat dry gently. Drizzle with orange
juice and maple syrup and stir in the Acai powder.
Roast the almond sticks in a frying pan until golden brown until they are
fragrant and allow to cool on a plate. Dust with a little cinnamon.
Stir quark and sugar until smooth.
Layer alternately the quark with the marinated blueberries in glasses
and garnish with the almonds.

9.13 Breakfast - Rice with fruits

Good to fight blood circulation disorders, thrombose, risk of embolism, high blood pressure, a headache, heart attack and stroke. Encourages blood build-up, promotes digestion, reduces Inflammation.
Cooking time approx. 10 min - 3 hours
Calories p. portion: 231
3 portions
Allergens: GHO

Quantity of ingredients:
Basic recipe for a rice soup (Congee) 6 cups / 500g. (yes)
Cow's milk (whole milk 3.5% fat) 1/2 to 1 cup / 80g. (yes)
Honey 1 table spoon / 10g. (yes)
Butter organic 1 table spoon / 15g. (yes)
Dates dried 1 table spoon / 15g. (yes)
Fig 1 table spoon / 15g. (yes)
Apple (sour) 1 piece / 200g. (recommended)
Hazelnuts 1/2 teaspoon / 5g. (recommended)
Almond 1/2 teaspoon / 5g. (recommended)
Cinnamon ground 1 pinch / 1g. (yes)

Cooking instructions:
Cook rice congee according to basic recipe or use pre-cooked.
Make it with the milk more fluid and sweet with honey.
Fry the fruits and nuts in butter and mix with the finished rice soup, add chopped dates, figs and the apple.

9.14 Breakfast with cheese

Good to fight weakness, stomach pressure, belching, diabetes, acute or chronic obstruction of the bowel, skin problems. Coffee supports urinating, stimulates appetite, detoxifying, increases blood glucose levels, harmonizes heart rhythm.
Cooking time approx. 10 min
Calories p. portion: 593
1 portions
Allergens: AGO

Quantity of ingredients:
Water 1 cup / 120g. (yes)
Coffee 2 teaspoons / 4g. (yes)
Whole grain bread 2 slices / 100g. (recommended)
Margarine 1/2 oz / 10g. (little)

Edam cheese 1 oz / 30g. (yes)
Strawberry jam 1/2 oz / 20g. (yes)
Curd cheese 20% 1/8 lbs - 2oz / 40g. (yes)

Cooking instructions:
Prepare coffee as usual. Avoid sugar or use sweetener. Cover the
bread slices with margarine and put the cheese and marmalade on the
breakfast table. Decorating decoratively increases your appetite.

9.15 Broccoli and Parmesan spread on toast bread

Good to fight loss of appetite, blood clotting, thyroid function, increase
Vitamin B12, strengthen immune system, good to fight belching,
diabetes, acute or chronic constipation, dissolves stagnation.
Cooking time approx. 15 min
Calories p. portion: 148
2 portions
Allergens: AG

Quantity of ingredients:
Broccoli 5/8 oz / 200g. (recommended)
Curd cheese 20% 3 oz / 80g. (yes)
Yogurt (natural, 1.5% fat) 1 table spoon / 10g. (yes)
Parmesan 2 table spoons / 15g. (yes)
Lemon peel 1/2 teaspoon / 1g. (yes)
Basil (fresh) 1 table spoon / 5g. (yes)
Chives 1 table spoon / 5g. (recommended)
Salt 1 pinch / 1g. (little)
Pepper (ground) 1 pinch / 0,3g. (yes)
Toast bread (whole grain) 6 slices / 24g. (yes)

Cooking instructions:
Cook broccoli in a sieve insert over steam for 8 minutes until firm. Finely
chop broccoli.
Mix the curd, yoghurt, parmesan and lemon peel well. Mix cheese
cream with broccoli, basil and chives. Season the spread with salt and
pepper. Serve on the crunchy toasted toast.

9.16 Broccoli cream soup

Strengthen your immune system, build and maintain healthy bones, teeth, hair and nails. Reduces blood pressure, strengthens immune system, prevents cancer, reduces radiation damage.
Cooking time approx. 30 min
Calories p. portion: 98
6 portions
Allergens: LO

Quantity of ingredients:
Olive oil 2 table spoons / 7g. (recommended)
Broccoli 1,1 lbs / 500g. (recommended)
Carrot 2 pieces / 150g. (recommended)
Potato 2 pieces / 120g. (yes)
Onion white 1 piece / 50g. (yes)
Water 1 cup / 50g. (yes)
Basic recipe for a vegetable soup (nutritious) 2 cup / 500g. (recommended)
White wine 1/2 cup / 125g. (little)
Sage 1 teaspoon / 2g. (yes)
Rosemary 1 teaspoon / 2g. (yes)
Pepper (ground) 1 pinch / 0,5g. (yes)
Salt 1 pinch / 1g. (little)

Cooking instructions:
Add the olive oil to the pan, add the washed and cut broccoli, diced carrots and potatoes, sauté for a short time, add the chopped onion, fill with water, enough water to cover the vegetables at least 3 finger breadths. Add bouillon, salt, add a little bit of white wine, add the seasoned sage and rosemary.
Heat till it boils and then simmer on a small fire for about 25 minutes. Season with pepper, if necessary season with sea salt. Purée the soup.

9.17 Bulgur with tomatoes and fresh herbs

Promotes digestion, helps to digest fat, supports urination, reduces blood pressure. Stimulates digestion, supports urination.
Cooking time approx. 30 min
Calories p. portion: 205
1 portions
Allergens: A

Quantity of ingredients:
Bulgur (cereals) 1 cup / 120g. (recommended)
Tomato 2 pieces / 70g. (recommended)
Rucola 2 table spoons / 16g. (recommended)
Pepper powder (hot) 1 pinch / 2g. (yes)
Olive oil 2 table spoons / 20g. (recommended)
Pepper (ground) 1 pinch / 0,5g. (yes)
Salt 1 pinch / 1g. (little)
Basil 4 leaves / 2g. (yes)
Thyme 1 Twig / 3g. (yes)
Lemon juice 1/2 piece / 10g. (yes)

Cooking instructions:
Put cold water in a pot, sprinkle in Bulgur and simmer. Stir in chopped tomatoes, fresh herbs like basil, thyme, arugula, a pinch of rose paprika, lemon juice, a dash of olive oil, a little ground pepper, some salt. Variant: add some mozzarella.
Recommendation: ideal morning meal in summer; also suitable as evening meal, especially for sleep disorders.

9.18 Carrot drink

Promotes spleen and liver, reduces blood pressure, strengthens immune system, prevents cancer, reduces radiation damage, diuretic, building up, eye-enhancing, detoxifying, nerve-strengthening.
Cooking time approx. 15 min
Calories p. portion: 143
1 portions
Allergens: H

Quantity of ingredients:
Millet flakes 1 table spoon / 10g. (recommended)
Carrot 7/8 lbs / 200g. (recommended)
Almond puree 1 teaspoon / 3g. (yes)
Honey 1/2 teaspoon / 2g. (yes)
Water / 50g. (yes)

Cooking instructions:
Sprinkle millet flakes with 50 ml of cold water and let it swell for 10 minutes.
Juice the fresh carrots or use 200 ml. carrot juice.
Puree the millet flakes, carrot juice, almond paste and honey with the blender.

9.19 Carrot Risotto

Strengthens immune system, prevents cancer, loss of appetite, flatulence, high blood pressure, depressions, diabetes, diarrhea, stimulates liver function, dissolves stagnation.
Cooking time approx. 45 min
Calories p. portion: 308
2 portions
Allergens: GL

Quantity of ingredients:
Olive oil 1/2 teaspoon / 5g. (recommended)
Onion (spring onion) 2 table spoons / 7g. (yes)
Nutmeg 1 pinch / 0,3g. (yes)
Parsley 1/2 bunch / 25g. (recommended)
Rice variety any 1/4 lbs - 4oz / 100g. (yes)
Carrot 5/8 lbs - 8oz / 250g. (recommended)
Basic recipe for a vegetable soup (nutritious) 1 cup / 280g. (recommended)
Fennel seeds ground 1/4 teaspoon / 1g. (yes)
Basil (fresh) 1/2 teaspoon / 2g. (yes)
Salt 1 pinch / 1g. (little)
Pepper (ground) 1 pinch / 0,3g. (yes)
Parmesan 1 table spoon / 10g. (yes)

Cooking instructions:
Heat the oil in a pan, fry the onions in a glassy and very soft manner. Add parsley, sauté briefly. Add rice, carrots and nutmeg, sauté briefly while stirring. Add the vegetable stock, season with fennel and basil, heat till it boils and cook for about 20 minutes until the rice and carrots are well. Stir from time to time and add some vegetable stock if necessary. The risotto should be slightly soupy. Just before the end of the cooking time mix in the white wine and simmer the risotto for a short while. Remove risotto from the heat, mix in Parmesan.

9.20 Cod soup with tomatoes

Promotes spleen and kidney; promotes watering. Improves blood circulation, improves medication effect, stimulates appetite, helps to digest fat, supports urination, stimulates liver function, detoxifying.
Cooking time approx. 30 min
Calories p. portion: 176
4 portions
Allergens: DLO

Quantity of ingredients:
Basic recipe for a fish soup 2 cup / 450g. (recommended)
Cod 5/8 lbs - 8oz / 250g. (recommended)
Onion (shallot) 1 piece / 20g. (yes)
Anise (Common Fennel) 1/2 teaspoon / 1g. (yes)
Ginger fresh 1/2 teaspoon / 1g. (yes)
Olive oil 1 teaspoon / 3g. (recommended)
Tomato 1 piece / 50g. (recommended)
White wine 1/2 cup / 125g. (little)
Salt 1 pinch / 0,5g. (little)
Pepper (ground) 1 pinch / 0,2g. (yes)
Parsley 1 table spoon (chopped) / 5g. (recommended)

Cooking instructions:
Fry the onion, anise and freshly grated ginger in oil.
Add finely chopped tomatoes and sauté. Add a little wine and fish soup.
Simmer gently for 10-15 minutes. Season with salt and pepper; Add the
cod pieces and heat gently. Garnish with parsley at the end.

9.21 Colorful rice dish

Strengthens immune system, good to fight diabetes, strengthens spleen
and stomach, strengthens blood, strengthens the muscles, tendons and
bones, promotes digestion, helps to digest fat, supports urination,
reduces blood pressure, dissolves stagnation.
Cooking time approx. 45 min
Calories p. portion: 437
3 portions
Allergens: L

Quantity of ingredients:
Olive oil 2 teaspoons / 20g. (recommended)
Onion (spring onion) 1 piece / 20g. (yes)
Beef meat 1/4 lbs - 4oz / 125g. (yes)
Rice (whole grain) 3 oz / 80g. (recommended)
Basic recipe for a vegetable soup (nutritious) 1 cup / 300g.
(recommended)
Celery root 1/8 lbs - 2oz / 50g. (yes)
Leek 1 piece / 100g. (recommended)
Beans (green, fresh) 3/8 lbs - 6oz / 150g. (yes)
Carrot 1 piece / 70g. (recommended)
Tomato 2 pieces / 100g. (recommended)

Salt 1 pinch / 0,5g. (little)
Pepper (ground) 1 pinch / 0,2g. (yes)
Peppers powder 1 pinch / 0,5g. (yes)
Herbs various 2 table spoons / 12g. (yes)

Cooking instructions:
Wash leek and carrots, clean and chop them. Dice the celery, slice the tomatoes.

Fry in a large, deep pan with oil, onion and minced meat.

Add brown rice and prepared vegetables (celery, leeks, beans, carrots, tomatoes). Braise briefly.

Season with salt, pepper and paprika. Add vegetable broth. Heat till it boils and cook over low heat for 20 to 30 minutes with the lid closed.

Sprinkle with fresh chopped herbs and serve.

9.22 Compote from blueberries

Laxative, antibacterial effect. Warms stomach and spleen, improves blood circulation.
Cooking time approx. 10 min
Calories p. portion: 49
1 portions
Allergens:

Quantity of ingredients:
Blueberry 1/4 lbs - 4oz / 100g. (recommended)
Water 1 cup / 120g. (yes)
Cinnamon ground 1 pinch / 0,1g. (yes)
Lemon peel 1 pinch / 1g. (yes)
Sugar cane sugar 1 teaspoon / 3g. (little)

Cooking instructions:
Cook the blueberries gently and sprinkle with sugar, cinnamon and grated lemon zest.

9.23 Cottage cheese with steamed fruit

Good to fight loss of appetite, promotes digestion, supports urination.
Cooking time approx. 20 min
Calories p. portion: 214
2 portions
Allergens: G

Quantity of ingredients:
Cottage cheese 3/4 lbs / 300g. (yes)
Apple (sour) 1 piece / 100g. (recommended)
Pear 1 piece / 100g. (recommended)

Cooking instructions:
Wash apples and pears well, do not peel, and chop small. In a pot with
steam filter, boil them al dente, remove and allow to cool down.
Serve the cheese, spread the fruit on it.

9.24 Couscous Salad

prevents cancer, forcing spleen, promotes digestion, stimulates liver
function, reduces blood pressure, strengthens immune system, reduces
radiation damage, diuretic.
Cooking time approx. 25 min
Calories p. portion: 338
3 portions
Allergens: A

Quantity of ingredients:
Water 1 cup / 100g. (yes)
Olive oil 1 table spoon / 15g. (recommended)
Couscous 5/8 oz / 200g. (recommended)
Lemon juice 2 table spoons / 30g. (yes)
Lemon peel 1 teaspoon / 2g. (yes)
Tomato 2 pieces / 80g. (recommended)
Cucumber 1/4 lbs - 4oz / 100g. (yes)
Carrot 1/4 lbs - 4oz / 100g. (recommended)
Parsley 1 Bunch / 100g. (recommended)
Chives 1 Bunch / 100g. (recommended)
Peppermint 3 twigs / 30g. (yes)

Cooking instructions:
Boil in a small saucepan 250 ml. water with salt and 1 tablespoon olive
oil. Add the couscous, take the stove in the front and let it swell covered

for 5 minutes. Put the couscous back on the stove and let it simmer for about 2 minutes with gentle stirring. If necessary, add 1 - 3 tbsp of hot water.

Mix the couscous with lemon juice, chopped lemon peel and 1 tbsp oil, season with salt and pepper and leave to set.

Add couscous with tomatoes, cucumber, parsley (all diced), carrots (grated), chives and mint (finely chopped). Season the couscous salad with lemon juice, salt and pepper.

9.25 Cranberry juice

Antibacterial, good to fight loss of appetite, arteriosclerosis, bladder infections, diarrhea, colds. Antipyretic, against free radicals, gout, diuretic, stomach ulcers, oral mucosa inflammation, rheumatism.
Cooking time approx. 5 min
Calories p. portion: 43
1 portions
Allergens:

Quantity of ingredients:
Cranberries 2 table spoons / 25g. (recommended)
Water 1 cup / 125g. (yes)
Honey 1 table spoon / 10g. (yes)

Cooking instructions:
Mix the cranberries with a little water with the blender to a pulp. Add the remaining water and sweeten with the honey.

9.26 Curry rice with raisins and nuts

Stops diarrhea, promotes digestion, appetizing, harmonizes the stomach, improves blood circulation, improves medication effect, stimulates appetite, detoxifies the skin, stimulates nerves, frees breathing, increases body temperature, promotes perspiration.
Cooking time approx. 30 min
Calories p. portion: 275
4 portions
Allergens: HO

Quantity of ingredients:
Sunflower oil 1 table spoon / 15g. (little)
Onion white 1 piece / 50g. (yes)
Curry 1/2 teaspoon / 2g. (yes)
Rice wild (nature rice) 1 cup / 120g. (recommended)

Salt 1 pinch / 1g. (little)
White wine 1/2 cup / 125g. (little)
Lemon Alternatively for white wine / g. (yes)
Peppers powder 1 pinch / 1g. (yes)
Apple (sweet) 2 pieces / 300g. (recommended)
Raisins 2 table spoons / 25g. (yes)
Walnuts 2 table spoons / 25g. (yes)
Water 6 cups / 500g. (yes)

Cooking instructions:
Heat oil in a pot; fry chopped onions until glassy; add the curry and let it foam for a short time; then fry the raw rice for a few minutes over a gentle heat, stirring constantly; Salt, a dash of white wine or lemon juice, rose paprika, sweet apples chopped, raisins, chopped, roasted nuts added; pour hot water on it until well covered; simmer until the rice is cooked.

Goes well with: carrot and fennel vegetables, legumes with boiled vegetables, sliced poultry with ginger and mushrooms.

9.27 Delicately spiced zucchini with tomatoes

Diuretic, promotes digestion, helps to digest fat, reduces blood pressure, dissolves stagnation, antioxidativ, supports urination, diuretic, warming the body from the inside, expands blood vessels.
Cooking time approx. 10 min
Calories p. portion: 203
4 portions
Allergens:

Quantity of ingredients:
Olive oil 1 table spoon / 20g. (recommended)
Onion white 2 pieces / 120g. (yes)
Zucchini 4 pieces / 800g. (yes)
Oregano dried 1 pinch / 1g. (yes)
Basil (fresh) 6-8 leaves / 3g. (yes)
Salt 1 pinch / 1g. (little)
Tomato 2 pieces / 120g. (recommended)
Rice (whole grain) 1 cup / 120g. (recommended)
Water 6 cups / 400g. (yes)
Salt 1 pinch / 1g. (little)

Cooking instructions:
In a hot pan, fry olive oil, finely chopped onions and finely chopped zucchini until half cooked. Add plenty of dried oregano. Salt and chop the tomatoes for a few minutes until the zucchini are tender but crisp. Add fresh basil as desired.

Variation: Put some sheep's cheese over the tomatoes and finish cooking with the lid closed.

Place the rice in salted water, heat till it boils and let it simmer over low heat for about 15 minutes.

9.28 Fast polenta with avocado and spring onion

Good to fight inflammations, swelling, pain. Forcing spleen and stomach, lets urine and bile juice flow, dissolves stagnation. Includes unsaturated fatty acids, antioxidativ.
Cooking time approx. 10 min
Calories p. portion: 450
2 portions
Allergens:

Quantity of ingredients:
Corn (fast polenta) 1 cup / 120g. (yes)
Water 1 1/2 cups / 240g. (yes)
Olive oil 1 table spoon / 15g. (recommended)
Salt 1 pinch / 1g. (little)
Pepper (ground) 1 pinch / 0,5g. (yes)
Lemon juice 1 dash / 3g. (yes)
Onion (spring onion) 2 pieces / 40g. (yes)
Avocado 1/2 piece / 150g. (recommended)
Turmeric (yellow root) 1 pinch / 1g. (recommended)
Basil (fresh) 1 teaspoon / 2g. (yes)

Cooking instructions:
Heat water, add oil, lemon and spices.
When the water boils, add the polenta while stirring constantly and cook for 2 minutes.
When the porridge becomes firm, the polenta is ready.
Add diced avocado and sliced spring onion to the polenta. Sprinkle fresh basil on it.

9.29 Fennel and potato gratin

Reduces inflammation, improves blood circulation, improves digestion, supports urination, lowers cholesterol, good to fight loss of appetite, flatulence, inflammatory bowel disease, heartburn. Forcing spleen, improves blood circulation.
Cooking time approx. 1 1/2 hours
Calories p. portion: 147
2 portions
Allergens: CGL

Quantity of ingredients:
Fennel 5/8 oz / 200g. (recommended)
Potato 1/4 lbs - 4oz / 125g. (yes)
Basic recipe for a vegetable soup (nutritious) 1/2 cup / 100g. (recommended)
Butter organic 1 teaspoon / 3g. (yes)
Rice flour 2 teaspoons / 6g. (yes)
Cream sour 10% 1 teaspoon / 3g. (yes)
Salt 1 pinch / 1g. (little)
Sugar cane sugar 1 pinch / 1g. (little)
Chicken yolk 1 piece / 10g. (little)
Pepper Cayenne 1 pinch / 0,5g. (yes)
Nutmeg 1 pinch / 0,5g. (yes)
Parsley 1 teaspoon / 2g. (recommended)
Chives 1 teaspoon / 3g. (recommended)
Parmesan 1 teaspoon / 3g. (yes)
Butter organic 1 teaspoon / 3g. (yes)

Cooking instructions:
Cook peeled potatoes and then let cool. Wash the fennel, cut off the stems and remove any outer leaves.
Hold back fennel greens and add it to the sauce with the other herbs later.
Steam the fennel tubers for about 15 - 20 minutes.
Then cut the potatoes and fennel into slices and place in layers in a greased baking dish.
Bring the liquid of fennel broth to the boil and bind it with flour.
Season with sea salt, cayenne pepper, sugar, nutmeg and sour cream. Allow to cool and alloy with egg yolk.
Spread the sauce over the casserole, sprinkle with parmesan and finely chopped parsley and chives. Bake at 200 °C / 392 °F in the oven for half an hour.

9.30 Fennel with roasted walnuts

Forcing spleen, detoxifying, reduces inflammation, improves blood circulation, improves medication effect, stimulates appetite, antioxidativ, promotes digestion, stimulates, dissolves stagnation.
Cooking time approx. 20 min
Calories p. portion: 342
4 portions
Allergens: HO

Quantity of ingredients:
Fennel 4 pieces / 800g. (recommended)
Nutmeg 1 pinch / 1g. (yes)
Ginger fresh 1/2 teaspoon / 1g. (yes)
Salt 1 pinch / 1g. (little)
White wine 1/2 cup / 125g. (little)
Peppers powder 1 pinch / 1g. (yes)
Olive oil 2 table spoons / 40g. (recommended)
Walnuts 2 table spoons / 35g. (yes)
Water 1 1/2 cups / 220g. (yes)
Corn Grease (Polenta) 1 cup / 120g. (yes)
Salt 1 pinch / 1g. (little)

Cooking instructions:
Heat very little water in a pot; Fry the fennel in strips. Add Nutmeg, a little grated ginger, add salt, a dash of white wine, rose paprika.
Simmer until the vegetables are cooked, but still crisp; stir in a little olive oil; sprinkle with roasted walnuts.

Stir the polenta into a pot of hot water, stirring constantly, until the polenta has the desired consistency. Salt.
Pull the polenta off the fire and let it swell for about 10 minutes.

9.31 Fennel-Rice Soup

Forcing spleen, relieves constipation, stimulates nerves, detoxifying, reduces inflammation, improves blood circulation.
Cooking time approx. 15-20 min
Calories p. portion: 156
2 portions
Allergens: EG

Quantity of ingredients:
Basic recipe for a rice soup (Congee) 1 cup / 300g. (yes)
Fennel 1/2 piece / 150g. (recommended)
Butter organic 1 table spoon / 15g. (yes)
Soy sauce 1 dash / 3g. (yes)

Cooking instructions:
Cook the fennel softly in the rice soup according to the basic recipe.
Before serving, add a piece of butter and some soy sauce.

9.32 Fine Russian borscht

Strengths spleen and stomach, strengthens the heart, stimulates
digestion, reduces blood pressure, strengthens immune system. For
strengthening after diseases. Good to fight bloating, cramping in
gastrointestinal complaints.
Cooking time approx. 30 min
Calories p. portion: 172
6 portions
Allergens: AGLO

Quantity of ingredients:
Red beet 5/8 oz / 200g. (yes)
Sunflower oil 1 table spoon / 10g. (little)
Onion (shallot) 2 pieces / 40g. (yes)
Carrot 2 pieces / 140g. (recommended)
Celery root 1 piece / 500g. (yes)
Parsley root 1 piece / 150g. (yes)
Leek 1/8 lbs - 2oz / 50g. (recommended)
Basic recipe for a vegetable soup (nutritious) 3 cups / 650g.
(recommended)
Bay leaf 1 Leaf / 0,2g. (yes)
Juniper berry 2 pieces / 2g. (yes)
Nutmeg 1 pinch / 1g. (yes)
Savoy cabbage / kale 5/8 oz / 200g. (yes)
Salt 1 pinch / 1g. (little)
Pepper (ground) 1 pinch / 0,5g. (yes)
Ground 1 pinch / 1g. (yes)
Red wine 1/2 cup / 125g. (little)
Sour cream 15% fat 1 table spoon / 10g. (yes)
Dill 1 teaspoon / 10g. (yes)
White bread (wheat bread) 6 slices / 120g. (little)

Cooking instructions:
Fry some beetroot in oil. Fry the onions, carrots, celery, parsley root and leek well in another pan. Add the stock and the wine; then add bay leaves, juniper berries and nutmeg and simmer for 15 minutes. Remove the bay leaf and puree everything.
Heat more broth separately, simmer the steamed beetroot in it. Add cabbage or white cabbage after half the cooking time and let it steep. At the end, add the pureed vegetables and season with salt, pepper, ground cumin and a little red wine. Garnish with some sour cream and finely chopped dill in the plate. Serve with a slice of white bread.

9.33 Fish soup with white wine, laurel and marjoram

Strengthens the kidneys, promotes watering, promotes spleen and liver, reduces blood pressure, improves blood circulation, improves medication effect, stimulates appetite, reduces blood pressure.
Cooking time approx. 45 min
Calories p. portion: 200
3 portions
Allergens: DLO

Quantity of ingredients:
Onion (spring onion) 2 pieces / 40g. (yes)
Garlic 1 clove / 2g. (recommended)
Basic recipe for a fish soup 2 cup / 500g. (recommended)
Carrot 1 piece / 60g. (recommended)
Parsnip 1 piece / 100g. (yes)
Celery root 1 slice / 60g. (yes)
Salt 1 pinch / 1g. (little)
Peppercorns 2 pieces / 1g. (yes)
Lemon 1/4 piece / 10g. (yes)
White wine 1/2 cup / 125g. (little)
Bay leaf 2 leaves / 1g. (yes)
Rosemary 1 teaspoon / 2g. (yes)
Chives 1 teaspoon (chopped) / 3g. (recommended)
Parsley 1 teaspoon (chopped) / 3g. (recommended)

Cooking instructions:
Fry the onion and garlic in oil until translucent. Add fish broth. Add the diced carrot, parsnip and celery. Season with salt and peppercorns. Simmer the soup on a low heat for 25 minutes.
Wash the fish, drizzle with lemon juice, divide into pieces and add to the soup with the wine, the bay leaves and the marjoram. Cook for 5 min on

low heat.
Add the chives and parsley and season the soup with the salt.

9.34 Fried apple

Good to fight acute or chronic constipation of the intestine, warming stomach and spleen, improves blood circulation. Good to fight kidney weakness, back pain and abdominal pain, impotence.
Cooking time approx. 30 min
Calories p. portion: 408
4 portions
Allergens: GH

Quantity of ingredients:
Apple (sour) 4 pieces / 500g. (recommended)
Hazelnuts 1/8 lbs - 2oz / 50g. (recommended)
Almond 1/8 lbs - 2oz / 50g. (recommended)
Cinnamon ground 1 pinch / 0,2g. (yes)
Vanilla sugar natural 1 package / 3g. (yes)
Cow's milk (whole milk 3.5% fat) 2 table spoons / 24g. (yes)
Sugar - icing sugar 2 table spoons / 36g. (little)
Cinnamon ground 1 pinch / 1g. (yes)
Yoghurt vanilla 3 cups / 750g. (yes)

Cooking instructions:
Wash the apples, cut off a lid, cut out the core casing with a teaspoon so that the apple remains a tight bottom.
Mix nuts, almonds, fructose, milk, vanilla sugar, cinnamon well. Fill into the apples. Put the covers back on.
Bake in preheated oven at 180 ° C for approx. 20 minutes.
Mix icing sugar and cinnamon.
Spread vanilla yoghurt on plate, place 1 baked apple on each, sprinkle with cinnamon-powdered sugar mixture. Serve hot immediately!

9.35 Fruit juice

Stops diarrhea, promotes digestion, appetizing, harmonizes the stomach, relieves pain, detoxifying, reduces blood pressure, strengthens immune system, prevents cancer, reduces radiation damage.
Cooking time approx. 10 min
Calories p. portion: 176
2 portions
Allergens:

Quantity of ingredients:
Orange 2 pieces / 150g. (recommended)
Apple (sweet) 4 pieces / 300g. (recommended)
Carrot 2 pieces / 150g. (recommended)
Honey 1 table spoon / 10g. (yes)

Cooking instructions:
Peel oranges and carrots. Cut all ingredients into cubes so that they fit into the juicer and juice. Sweet with honey.

9.36 Grilled salmon steaks with cauliflower and potatoes

Improves digestion, regenerates skin, supports urination, lowers cholesterol, supports digestion.
Cooking time approx. 30 min
Calories p. portion: 330
4 portions
Allergens: D

Quantity of ingredients:
Garlic 1 clove / 1g. (recommended)
Onion (shallot) 1/2 piece / 5g. (yes)
Lemon juice 1 dash / 1g. (yes)
Salt 1 pinch / 1g. (little)
Cauliflower 1 piece / 500g. (yes)
Olive oil 2 table spoons / 20g. (recommended)
Garlic 1 clove / 1g. (recommended)
Water 2/3 cup / g. (yes)
Parsley 2 table spoons / 15g. (recommended)
Potato 1,1 lbs / 500g. (yes)
Salt 1 pinch / 1g. (little)
Salmon 4 pieces (steaks) / 500g. (yes)
Lemon 1/2 piece / 2g. (yes)

Cooking instructions:
Garlic shallots mixture:
Finely squeeze the garlic, finely chop the shallots, add a dash of lemon juice and salt and stir. Mix with a little oil to a paste.

Cauliflower:
Cut the cauliflower into pieces.

Heat the oil in a heavy saucepan and fry the crushed garlic for a short time.
Add the cauliflower pieces and turn in the oil. Add a little water and cook until the cauliflower is firm. Strain the cauliflower and cook the remaining water until a thick sauce remains. Add the cauliflower and crush it roughly with a wooden spoon. Add the chopped parsley and salt.

Potatoes:
Cook the potato in a saucepan with plenty of water, strain and peel.

Salmon Steak:
Preheat the oven at about 180°C/356°F. Rub in the salmon slices with the garlic-scarlet mixture and grill as close as possible to the heat source for 4 to 8 minutes from both sides. You are done when the meat is easy to divide when you pierce with a fork.

Serve and sprinkle with lemon slices and the chopped parsley.

9.37 Grilled tomatoes with cheese filling

Promotes digestion, helps to digest fat, supports urination, reduces blood pressure, stimulates digestion.
Cooking time approx. 30 min
Calories p. portion: 470
2 portions
Allergens: ACG

Quantity of ingredients:
Tomato 8 pieces / 200g. (recommended)
Feta cheese 0,2 lbs / 75g. (yes)
Fresh cheese 0,2 lbs / 75g. (yes)
Chicken egg 1 piece / 60g. (little)
Olive oil 1 table spoon / 12g. (recommended)
Basil (fresh) 1 table spoon / 6g. (yes)
Salt 1 pinch / 1g. (little)
Pepper (ground) 1 pinch / 0,5g. (yes)
Olives 1 oz / 30g. (yes)
Rucola 1/4 lbs / 100g. (recommended)
White bread (wheat bread) 4 slices / 80g. (little)

Cooking instructions:
Hollow out tomatoes generously. Put in a casserole dish.
Mix cheese, olive oil, egg, chopped basil and flour. Season with salt and pepper and fill in the tomatoes.
Bake in the preheated oven at 210 degrees on the middle rail for 15 minutes, then switch on the oven grill and grill for a further 3 minutes (without circulating air).
Stone the olives and chop and sprinkle on the tomatoes.
Garnish tomatoes with rocket and serve with white bread.

9.38 Halibut with tomato and garlic sauce

Promotes digestion, helps to digest fat, supports urination, reduces blood pressure, good to fight rheumatism, flatulence, bladder weakness, anemia, high blood pressure, depressions, diabetes, diarrhea. Valuable omega-3 fatty acids.
Cooking time approx. 45 min
Calories p. portion: 319
5 portions
Allergens: D

Quantity of ingredients:
Rice variety any 1 cup / 120g. (yes)
Water 6 cups / 240g. (yes)
Salt 1 pinch / 1g. (little)
Halibut (Flatfish) 2,2 lbs / 800g. (recommended)
Salt 1 pinch / 1g. (little)
Pepper (ground) 1 pinch / 0,5g. (yes)
Lemon juice 1 dash / 2g. (yes)
Bay leaf 2 pieces / 2g. (yes)
Lemon 1 piece / 30g. (yes)
Garlic 8 pieces / 10g. (recommended)
Thyme dried 1 table spoon / 5g. (yes)
Olives 0,2 lbs / 75g. (yes)
Tomato 4 pieces / 200g. (recommended)
Salt 1 pinch / 1g. (little)
Pepper (ground) 1 pinch / 0,5g. (yes)

Cooking instructions:
Cook rice with salted water (1:3).
Rinse the fish under running cold water, dab with kitchen paper and rub with salt, pepper and lemon juice.
Place the fish fillets in a casserole dish with pieces of bay leaf.

Wash the lemon hot and cut into slices, peel and halve the garlic.
Sprinkle the olives and the thyme over them.
Brew the tomatoes with hot water, skin and chop.

Mix all ingredients, season with salt and pepper and distribute around the fish.

Cook everything at 200°C/392°F for about 20 minutes.
Serve with the rice.

9.39 Indian Dal soup

Strengthens heart and kidney, diuretic, calms the stomach, promotes digestion, reduces blood pressure, strengthens immune system, improves blood circulation, strengthens the muscles. Strengthens gastrointestinal function, expands blood vessels.
Cooking time approx. 30 min
Calories p. portion: 256
2 portions
Allergens: EN

Quantity of ingredients:
Lentils 3/8 lbs - 6oz / 175g. (yes)
Sesame oil 2 table spoons / 30g. (little)
Carrot 1 piece / 100g. (recommended)
Onion (shallot) 1 piece / 15g. (yes)
Water 1 1/2 cups / 200g. (yes)
Ginger fresh 2 slices / 1g. (yes)
Salt 1 pinch / 0,5g. (little)
Soy sauce 1 teaspoon / 3g. (yes)
Parsley 1 teaspoon (chopped) / 3g. (recommended)
Thyme 1 teaspoon / 3g. (yes)
Basil 1 table spoon / 5g. (yes)

Cooking instructions:
Soak the lentils overnight.
in a hot pot, carrot, onion and a little ginger fry, pour water. Add the lentils and cook until soft. Add salt or soy sauce and cook for another 10 minutes.
Stir in parsley before serving; Sprinkle thyme or basil over it.
Variant: Other herbs such as sage, rosemary or lovage allow a variety of flavors.

9.40 Japanese algae soup

Reduces blood pressure, strengthens immune system, prevents cancer, reduces radiation damage. Promotes digestion. Detoxifying and stimulates the immune system.
Cooking time approx. 20 min
Calories p. portion: 47
3 portions
Allergens:

Quantity of ingredients:
Wakame 1 oz / 25g. (yes)
Water 2 cup / 450g. (yes)
Onion (shallot) 1-2 pcs. / 30g. (yes)
Radish (white, green, purple-red) 1/8 lbs - 2oz / 50g. (recommended)
Carrot 2 pieces / 180g. (recommended)
Miso 2 table spoons / 20g. (yes)
Parsley 2 table spoons / 20g. (recommended)
Onion (spring onion) 1 table spoon (sliced)

Cooking instructions:
Soak wakame in water for a few minutes, remove and bring the water to the boil. Add finely chopped onions and wakame, radishes and carrots, cut into thin strips, and simmer for another 10 minutes. Dissolve miso in a little cooled cooking water and add it at the end. Sprinkle with parsley and spring onions.

9.41 Kohlrabi in chervil sauce with potatoes

Reduces inflammation, lowers cholesterol, diuretic, conducts bowel winds, strengthens immune system, prevents cancer, promotes weight loss. Good to fight loss of appetite, flatulence, high blood pressure, depressions, diabetes, diarrhea.
Cooking time approx. 1 hour
Calories p. portion: 188
4 portions
Allergens: GL

Quantity of ingredients:
Potato 6 pieces / 450g. (yes)
Basic recipe for a vegetable soup (nutritious) 1 cup / 300g. (recommended)
Potato 1/4 lbs - 4oz / 100g. (yes)
Nutmeg 1 pinch / 0,2g. (yes)

Lemon peel 1/2 teaspoon / 2g. (yes)
Ginger fresh 1/2 teaspoon / 2g. (yes)
Lovage 1/2 teaspoon / 2g. (yes)
Kohlrabi 3/4 lbs / 300g. (recommended)
Salt 1 pinch / 1g. (little)
Pepper (ground) 1 pinch / 0,2g. (yes)
Sour cream 15% fat 2 table spoons / 30g. (yes)
Chervil dried 1 Bunch / 80g. (yes)

Cooking instructions:
Boil the potatoes in salted water.
Bring half of the vegetable stock to boil. Add the diced potatoes, nutmeg, lemon zest, ginger and lovage. Cover the potatoes and cook for about 10 minutes until soft and puree them with a blender until they are smooth.
Bring remaining vegetable stock to boil. Cut kohlrabi into cubes and add, cover and cook for about 8 minutes. Stir in the potato sauce and heat everything briefly.
Puree with the mixing stick chervil and sour cream. Mix the chervil cream with the kohlrabi vegetables.
Serve with the cooked, peeled potatoes.

9.42 Lasagne with tofu cream

Harmonizes spleen and stomach, reduces Flatulence, protects the digestive system. Good to fight lack of appetite, flatulence, inflammatory bowel disease, stomach ulcers, rheumatism, heartburn.
Cooking time approx. 45 min
Calories p. portion: 301
4 portions
Allergens: ACEG

Quantity of ingredients:
Soy Tofu 7/8 lbs / 400g. (recommended)
Chicken egg 2 pieces / 100g. (little)
Onion white 2 pieces / 120g. (yes)
Tomato 1/4 lbs - 4oz / 100g. (recommended)
Oregano dried 1 pinch / 1g. (yes)
Marjoram 1 pinch / 1g. (yes)
Peppers powder 1 pinch / 1g. (yes)
Salt 1 pinch / 1g. (little)
Noodles (wheat, lasagne) with egg 3/8 lbs - 6oz / 150g. (yes)
Edam cheese 1/8 lbs - 2oz / 50g. (yes)

Cooking instructions:
Tofu cream: Mix tofu with eggs, onions, small tomatoes, oregano, marjoram, peppers and some sea salt put into a smooth mass using a kitchen machine with a knife or a blender.

Lasagne: Place 1/5 of the tofu cream in a casserole dish (25x15cm), cover with 3 lasagna leaves, repeat this process twice, and then finish the last fifth of the tofu cream over the pastry plates. Sprinkle with a little grated Edam and bake in the oven at 175°C/347°F for about 1/2 hour.

9.43 Leek and potato gratin

Reduces inflammation, improves digestion, regenerates skin, supports urination, lowers cholesterol, promotes sweating, dissolves stagnation.
Cooking time approx. 1 hour
Calories p. portion: 368
4 portions
Allergens: CGL

Quantity of ingredients:
Potato 1,1 lbs / 500g. (yes)
Leek 1,1 lbs / 500g. (recommended)
Apple (sour) 1 piece / 200g. (recommended)
Créme fraiche cheese 1/4 lbs - 4oz / 125g. (yes)
Basic recipe for a vegetable soup (nutritious) 1/4 cup / 20g. (recommended)
Chicken yolk 1 piece / 20g. (little)
Emmental cheese 2 table spoons / 20g. (yes)
Salt 1 pinch / 1g. (little)
Pepper (ground) 1 pinch / 0,5g. (yes)

Cooking instructions:
Wash the potatoes, peel, cut into very thin slices and pat dry. Place half in a flat greased baking dish.
Clean and wash leeks and cut into fine rings. Wash apple, peel and cut into thin slices. Spread the leek rings and apple slices on top. Put the remaining potato slices on top.
Mix crème fraîche, egg yolk, grated Emmentaler, salt and pepper, if necessary add some vegetable stock and pour over the casserole.
Bake at 200°C/392°F in the oven for about 45 to 50 minutes until golden brown. Cover with parchment paper after 30 minutes to prevent the burr from drying out.

9.44 Lentil and chestnut soup with curry

Reduces blood pressure, strengthens immune system, prevents cancer, reduces radiation damage, forcing spleen, dissolves stagnation, promotes weight loss. Good to fight immunodeficiency, loss of appetite, flatulence, high blood pressure, depressions, diabetes, diarrhea.
Cooking time approx. 45 min
Calories p. portion: 176
4 portions
Allergens: LO

Quantity of ingredients:
Lentils red 3/8 lbs - 6oz / 150g. (yes)
Chestnuts 3/8 lbs - 6oz / 150g. (recommended)
Olive oil 1 table spoon / 10g. (recommended)
Curry 2 teaspoons / 8g. (yes)
Turmeric (yellow root) 1 teaspoon / 2g. (recommended)
Basic recipe for a vegetable soup (nutritious) 2 cup / 500g. (recommended)
White wine 1/2 cup / 125g. (little)
Salt (herbal) 1 pinch / 1g. (little)
Anise (Common Fennel) 1 pinch / 1g. (yes)
Cardamom 1 pinch / 0,5g. (yes)
Cardamom 1 pinch / 1g. (yes)
Parsley 2 table spoons / 6g. (recommended)

Cooking instructions:
Add the olive oil to a pan, sauté the chestnuts, sprinkle with the curry, add the lentils and season with vegetable stock, add a little white wine, mix in the curcuma, simmer for about 20 minutes (until the chestnuts are tender).
Then puree the soup.
Taste with a pinch of anise, cardamom and herbal salt. At the end, sprinkle finely chopped parsley over it.

9.45 Lettuce with fresh cheese

The bitter substances have diuretic effect and promote the blood circulation in the digestive area. Mustard improves thyroid function, relieves rheumatism symptoms.
Cooking time approx. 5 min
Calories p. portion: 802
1 portions
Allergens: AFM

Quantity of ingredients:
Leaf salads (bitter) 2 portions / 60g. (yes)
Fresh cheese from soya 3/8 lbs - 6oz / 150g. (yes)
Mustard 1 knife tip / 1g. (recommended)
Lemon juice 1 dash / 3g. (yes)
Salt 1 pinch / 1g. (little)
Pepper (ground) 1 pinch / 0,5g. (yes)
Herbs various 2 teaspoons / 4g. (yes)
Black caraway 1 pinch / 1g. (yes)
Whole grain bread 2 slices / 40g. (recommended)

Cooking instructions:
Wash lettuce and finely pluck.
Mix 150 ml cream cheese, splashes of mustard, splashes of lemon
juice, 1 clove of garlic, chopped fresh herbs, pinch of pepper and
crushed black cumin and pour over. Serve with wholemeal bread.

9.46 Melanzani with olive oil and turmeric

improves blood circulation, reduces inflammation, relieves pain,
promotes digestion, helps to digest fat, supports urination, reduces
blood pressure.
Cooking time approx. 30 min
Calories p. portion: 432
2 portions
Allergens: A

Quantity of ingredients:
Aubergine 2 pieces / 300g. (yes)
Olive oil 4 table spoons / 60g. (recommended)
Tomato 4 pieces / 200g. (recommended)
Turmeric (yellow root) 1/2 teaspoon / 1g. (recommended)
Ground 1 pinch / 1g. (yes)
Salt 1 pinch / 1g. (little)
White bread (wheat bread) 4 slices / 80g. (little)

Cooking instructions:
Cut the melanzani into slices and spread them with the tomatoes on a
baking tray. Sprinkle with olive oil and then with turmeric, caraway and
salt. Bake them in the tube 20 min.
Serve with the white bread.

9.47 Milk rice vanilla - with cherries

Little laxative, improves blood circulation, reduces inflammation, moisturizer dry skin. Strengthens spleen and stomach, strengthens the muscles. Antioxidant.
Cooking time approx. 20 min
Calories p. portion: 394
4 portions
Allergens: GO

Quantity of ingredients:
Cow's milk (1.5% fat) 3,3 lbs / 1400g. (yes)
Rice round grain 5/8 oz / 200g. (yes)
Pudding powder vanilla 1 package / 5g. (yes)
Cherry compote 5/8 oz / 200g. (yes)
Acai powder 2 teaspoons / 6g. (recommended)
Sugar white 1 table spoon / 9g. (little)
Salt 1 pinch / 1g. (little)

Cooking instructions:
Put milk in a saucepan and heat till it boil. Add the rice and remove from the heat. Leave 10 min. Put again on a small flame, add a pinch of salt and about 2 tablespoons of sugar. Add the packet of vanilla pudding. Carefully, with a small cooker setting, bring to the boil while stirring.

Pour the juice from the cherries.

Depending on your hunger, place the rice on a plate, arrange the cherries nicely and sprinkle 1-2 teaspoons of acai powder over the cherries with a powdered sugar sieve.

9.48 Millet with shiitake mushrooms and avocado

Anti-inflammatory, good to fight swelling and pain, promotes spleen and kidney, diuretic, stimulates digestion, building up, eye-enhancing, detoxifying, nerve-strengthening, building up.
Cooking time approx. 20 min
Calories p. portion: 560
2 portions
Allergens: G

Quantity of ingredients:
Millet 1 cup / 120g. (little)
Water 1 1/2 cups / 200g. (yes)
Shiitake, dried 1 oz / 25g. (yes)
Ginger fresh 1/2 teaspoon / 2g. (yes)
Pepper (ground) 1 pinch / 0,5g. (yes)
Salt 1 pinch / 1g. (little)
Parsley 1 table spoon / 7g. (recommended)
Peppers powder 1 pinch / 1g. (yes)
Butter organic 1 table spoon / 15g. (yes)
Avocado 1 piece / 200g. (recommended)
Lemon juice 1 dash / 3g. (yes)
Rucola 2 handful / 30g. (recommended)

Cooking instructions:
In a saucepan with hot water, sprinkle the millet, add in strips cut
shiitake mushrooms and some ginger and simmer; add a pinch of
ground pepper, a little salt, plenty of parsley, a pinch of rose pepper, stir
in a piece of butter.
In the meantime: place ½ peeled avocado per serving on one half of the
plate: sprinkle with a little ground pepper, a small pinch of salt; drizzle
with lemon juice; sprinkle a little chopped rocket or rose paprika over it.
Put the millet dish on the other half of the plate.

9.49 Miso soup with tofu

Vitamins, minerals and secondary plant active ingredients, invigorating,
detoxifying, strengthens immune system, promotes digestion, forcing
spleen, containing enzymes, reduces flatulence, alginic acid detoxifies
the bowel, dissolves stagnation.
Cooking time approx. 5 min
Calories p. portion: 51
3 portions
Allergens: E

Quantity of ingredients:
Wakame 1 piece / 5g. (yes)
Miso 3-4 table spoons / 30g. (yes)
Soy Tofu 1/8 lbs - 2oz / 50g. (recommended)
Water 2 cup / 500g. (yes)
Soy sauce 1 dash / 3g. (yes)
Onion (spring onion) 1/2 teaspoon / 6g. (yes)

Cooking instructions:
Boil soybean seedlings, wakame algae and diced tofu for 5 minutes.
Put the miso paste in the soup plate and slowly pour over the soup.
Season with Tamari sauce. Sprinkle with cutted spring onion.

9.50 Muesli with Acai Powder

Fibre-rich, relieves constipation, strengthens immune system, digestive-regulating, forcing spleen, promotes weight loss. Good to fight immunodeficiency, loss of appetite.
Cooking time approx. 2 hours and more
Calories p. portion: 391
1 portions
Allergens: AGH

Quantity of ingredients:
Muesli 2 table spoons / 20g. (yes)
Oat flakes (whole grain) 2 table spoons / 20g. (yes)
Yogurt (natural, 3.5% fat) 6 table spoons / 80g. (yes)
Lemon 1 table spoon / 10g. (yes)
Acerola fruit nectar or powder 1/2 teaspoon / 1g. (recommended)
Acai powder 1 teaspoon / 2g. (recommended)
Apple (sour) 1 piece / 170g. (recommended)
Hazelnuts 1 table spoon / 10g. (recommended)

Cooking instructions:
Soak oatmeal in the yogurt for several hours in the fridge. Grate nuts, add lemon juice, acerola and acai powder, grated apple. For sweets, raisins can be used.

9.51 Noodles with vegetable and tomato sauce

Protects the digestive system. Detoxifying, Good to fight loss of appetite, flatulence, inflammatory bowel disease, obesity, gout, stomach ulcers, stomach cramps, rheumatism, heartburn, twelffinger intestinal ulcers, promotes digestion, helps to digest fat.
Cooking time approx. 45 min
Calories p. portion: 562
2 portions
Allergens: ACG

Quantity of ingredients:
Tomato 1/4 lbs - 4oz / 125g. (recommended)
Carrot 1 piece / 80g. (recommended)
Zucchini 1 piece / 80g. (yes)
Olive oil 1 table spoon / 15g. (recommended)
Onion (shallot) 1 piece / 20g. (yes)
Oregano dried 1 pinch / 1g. (yes)
Salt 1 pinch / 1g. (little)
Pepper (ground) 1 pinch / 0,2g. (yes)
Noodles (wheat) with egg 5/8 oz / 200g. (yes)
Olive oil 1 table spoon / 10g. (recommended)
Créme fraiche cheese 2 table spoons / 30g. (yes)

Cooking instructions:
Boil the tomatoes with a little water, drain and collect the juice, cut the tomatoes into pieces.
Roughly grate zucchini and carrot. Heat olive oil in a pot. Steam shallots very soft. Add tomatoes, season with oregano, salt and pepper. Simmer tomatoes to a thick sauce.
Bring plenty of salted water to boil, cook the wholegrain noodles until firm. In the cooking time of the pasta, heat in a pan olive oil. Fry the carrots while stirring, lightly salt. Add zucchini, sauté briefly while stirring. The vegetables should be soft with a bite.
Drain pasta, mix with créme fraiche, season with salt and pepper. Garnish with the tomato sauce.

9.52 Oat flakes with aromatic spices

Stops diarrhea, promotes digestion, appetizing, harmonizes the stomach, relieves diarrhea, strengthens immune system, detoxifying and stimulating the immune system.
Cooking time approx. 25 min
Calories p. portion: 280
3 portions
Allergens: AH

Quantity of ingredients:
Oat flakes (whole grain) 1 cup / 125g. (yes)
Walnuts 1 table spoon / 15g. (yes)
Hazelnuts 1 table spoon / 15g. (recommended)
Water 1 1/2 cups / 240g. (yes)
Wakame 1 inch / 2g. (yes)
Apple (sweet) 1 piece / 220g. (recommended)

Cardamom 3-4 capsules / 2g. (yes)
Lemon Balm (fresh) 3-4 leaves / 3g. (recommended)
Acerola fruit nectar or powder 1 teaspoon / 2g. (recommended)

Cooking instructions:
Roast oatmeal and nuts. Add hot water. Add cardamom, wakame and cook for 20 min. Add grated apple, acerola and lemon herb.

9.53 Oatmeal soup with spring onion and carrots

Reduces blood pressure, strengthens immune system, , stimulates digestion, stimulates appetite, dissolves stagnation.
Cooking time approx. 30 min
Calories p. portion: 135
3 portions
Allergens: AG

Quantity of ingredients:
Oat 6 table spoons / 48g. (yes)
Carrot 2 pieces / 200g. (recommended)
Butter organic 1 table spoon / 15g. (yes)
Nutmeg 1 pinch / 1g. (yes)
Lovage 1 stem / 15g. (yes)
Onion (spring onion) 2 pieces / 40g. (yes)
Water 2 cup / 480g. (yes)

Cooking instructions:
Roast the oats in butter, add salt and spices, pour in water and heat till it boils. After 10 min. add the grated carrots and lovage, cook for 10 minutes. Finely add chopped onion.

9.54 Pear juice

Promotes digestion, supports urination.
Cooking time approx. 5 min
Calories p. portion: 180
2 portions
Allergens:

Quantity of ingredients:
Pear 3 pieces / 600g. (recommended)

Cooking instructions:
Peel pears thinly (vitamins under the skin) and core. Juice in the juicer.

9.55 Pear with candy sugar and sticky rice

Promotes digestion, supports urination. Strengthens spleen and stomach.
Cooking time approx. 50 min
Calories p. portion: 217
4 portions
Allergens: GH

Quantity of ingredients:
Pear 2 pieces / 300g. (recommended)
Sugar candy white 1 teaspoon / 4g. (little)
Lemon 1/2 piece / 10g. (yes)
Water 2 cup / 500g. (yes)
Acerola fruit nectar or powder 1 teaspoon / 2g. (recommended)
Rice sticky 1 cup / 120g. (yes)
Water 3 cups / 300g. (yes)
Almond puree 2 table spoons / 20g. (yes)
Cream (30% fat) 2 table spoons / 20g. (little)
Maple syrup 1-2 table spoon / 15g. (recommended)
Cinnamon ground 1 pinch / 1g. (yes)

Cooking instructions:
Simmer halved unpeeled organic pear (with seeds) with sugar candy and half of the lemon covered approx. 20min. After cooling, add acerola. Cook the rice with water (1: 3) about 45min. Cover and cook on the lowest heat. Form the rice into small balls. Arrange the pears with the juice with the rice balls. Decorate the pears with almond purée and whipped cream. If you like it sweeter, sweeten with maple syrup. Sprinkle with cinnamon.

9.56 Potato cream with herbs and fresh cheese

Good to fight loss of appetite, constipation, bloating and nausea. Improves digestion, supports urination, prevents cancer, forcing spleen, dissolves stagnation, relaxing and reassuring.
Cooking time approx. 25 min
Calories p. portion: 217
2 portions
Allergens: G

Quantity of ingredients:
Potato (mealy) 5/8 lbs - 8oz / 250g. (yes)
Fresh cheese 3 oz / 80g. (yes)

Yogurt (natural, 1.5% fat) 2 table spoons / 45g. (yes)
Chives 1/2 bunch / 50g. (recommended)
Basil (fresh) 1 teaspoon / 4g. (yes)
Parsley 1 teaspoon / 4g. (recommended)
Dill 1/2 teaspoon / 2g. (yes)
Salt 1 pinch / 1g. (little)
Black caraway 1 pinch / 0,5g. (yes)
Pepper (ground) 1 pinch / 0,5g. (yes)

Cooking instructions:
Softly steam the potatoes in the pan, peel them and press through the potato press.
Mix cream cheese, yoghurt and herbs under the potatoes, season with salt, crushed black cumin and pepper.

9.57 Potato-basil soup

Reduces inflammation, improves digestion, supports urination, lowers cholesterol, reduces blood pressure, strengthens immune system, prevents cancer, reduces radiation damage, antioxidativ, dissolves stagnation.
Cooking time approx. 25 min
Calories p. portion: 96
4 portions
Allergens: L

Quantity of ingredients:
Water 2 cups / 450g. (yes)
Potato 4 pieces / 200g. (yes)
Carrot 2 pieces / 100g. (recommended)
Celery root 1 piece / 500g. (yes)
Pepper (ground) 1 pinch / 0,5g. (yes)
Ground 1 pinch / 1g. (yes)
Garlic 1 clove / 3g. (recommended)
Salt 1 pinch / 1g. (little)
Lemon 1 teaspoon / 3g. (yes)
Basil (fresh) 1 Bunch / 50g. (yes)
Peppers powder 1 pinch / 1g. (yes)
Sugar cane sugar 1 pinch / 1g. (little)
Olive oil 1 table spoon / 10g. (recommended)

Cooking instructions:
Peeled and chopped 4 medium potatoes in a pot of hot water and 2
chopped medium carrots, a piece of celery root, a pinch of pepper, a
pinch of ground cumin, crushed a small clove of garlic, a pinch of salt, 1
teaspoon of lemon juice, simmer until the Vegetables is soft.

Add 1 bunch finely chopped basil into one half of the soup and puree
everything; stir in the other half of the basil; with rose paprika, a pinch of
whole cane sugar, 1 tablespoon of olive oil or butter, freshly ground
pepper, salt to taste.

9.58 Puréed banana

Eat 2 times a day, regulates gastrointestinal function
Cooking time approx. 7 min
Calories p. portion: 144
1 portions
Allergens:

Quantity of ingredients:
Banana 1 piece / 150g. (recommended)

Cooking instructions:
Mix the banana with the fork or purée with a blender. Leave to brown for
at least 5 minutes.

9.59 Quick flakes with compote or jam

Relieves pain, detoxifying, bactericide. Dissolves stones. Promotes
digestion, nourishes bones and tendons, warms kidneys and spleen,
forcing spleen, neutralizes Flatulence, controls excessive urge to
urinate, helps to fight digestive weakness.
Cooking time approx. 5 min
Calories p. portion: 189
2 portions
Allergens: H

Quantity of ingredients:
Quinoa 5-7 table spoons / 50g. (yes)
Water 1 cup / 250g. (yes)
Compote (fruits of the season) 1 cup / 100g. (recommended)
Walnuts 1 table spoon (grated) / 8g. (yes)

Olive oil 1 table spoon / 10g. (recommended)
Honey 2 table spoons / 20g. (yes)
Vanilla 1 pinch / 0,2g. (yes)
Anise (Common Fennel) 1 pinch / 0,2g. (yes)
Cardamom 1 pinch / 0,2g. (yes)

Cooking instructions:
Put the quinoa flakes in a pan and add water. Boil for 3-5 minutes, pull from the fire, add nuts and compote. Add a dash of oil. Sweeten as needed with honey, whole cane sugar or agave syrup.

Spices and aromas: vanilla, anise, fennel or coriander, cardamom, a little chili.

Winter: apple compote, pear compote, fruit jam.
Summer: plum compote, apricot compote.

9.60 Quick zucchini soup

Diuretic, supports urination. Strengthens gastrointestinal function, expands blood vessels, prevents cancer, prevents diseases (in the elderly). Stimulates liver function, detoxifying.
Cooking time approx. 10 min
Calories p. portion: 42
4 portions
Allergens:

Quantity of ingredients:
Zucchini 2-3 pieces / 500g. (yes)
Onion white 1 piece / 50g. (yes)
Corn germ oil 2 table spoons / 6g. (little)
Parsley 1 table spoon / 7g. (recommended)
Chives 1 teaspoon / 3g. (recommended)
Water 2 cup / 400g. (yes)

Cooking instructions:
Fry chopped onion in oil. Add sliced zucchini and sauté well. Pour with water. Chop parsley and chives, add and puree everything.

9.61 Radish, apple and yogurt fresh food

Stops diarrhea, promotes digestion, appetizing, detoxifying, supports urination, reduces thirst, prevents cancer, strengthens body cells, dissolves stagnation.
Cooking time approx. 10 min
Calories p. portion: 77
2 portions
Allergens: G

Quantity of ingredients:
Yogurt (natural, 3.5% fat) 5 table spoons / 50g. (yes)
Lemon juice 1/2 teaspoon / 2g. (yes)
Salt 1 pinch / 0,5g. (little)
Pepper white (ground) 1 pinch / 0,1g. (yes)
Radish (white, green, purple-red) 1/4 lbs - 4oz / 100g. (recommended)
Apple (sweet) 1 piece / 150g. (recommended)
Parsley 2 table spoons / 18g. (recommended)

Cooking instructions:
Mix yoghurt with lemon juice, salt and white pepper.

Wash radish and apple, peel and finely grate. Mix with the yoghurt sauce, let it pass briefly. Sprinkle with chopped parsley.

9.62 Red lentils with avocado and radish

Inflammations, promotes digestion, detoxifying, supports urination, reduces thirst. Strengthens heart and kidney, diuretic, calms the stomach, promotes digestion.
Cooking time approx. 20 min
Calories p. portion: 269
3 portions
Allergens: N

Quantity of ingredients:
Ginger fresh 2 slices / 2g. (yes)
Water 1 1/2 cups / 200g. (yes)
Lentils red 1 cup peeled / 100g. (yes)
Wakame 1 inch / 1g. (yes)
Salt 1 pinch / 0,5g. (little)
Lemon juice 1 dash / 1g. (yes)

Curcuma 1 pinch / 0,3g. (yes)
Avocado 1 piece / 300g. (recommended)
Pepper (ground) 1 pinch / 0,2g. (yes)
Pepper powder (hot) 1 pinch / 0,2g. (yes)
Sesame oil 1 dash / 1g. (little)
Radish (white, green, purple-red) 1 cup / 100g. (recommended)

Cooking instructions:
Put in a pot with water, some chopped ginger, peeled red lentils, a piece of wakame or a small amount of hijiki and simmer until the lentils are soft. Season with salt, lemon juice and turmeric.

Meanwhile: place half an avocado per serving on one-third of the plate: add ground pepper, a pinch of salt, a little lemon juice, a pinch of sweet pepper and a little sesame oil.

Put the grated radish on the second plate third.

Fill the lentil dish into the last third of the plate.
Variant: Use radish slices instead of radishes.

9.63 Reissue soup with fresh fruits

Diuretic, warming the body from the inside, expands blood vessels, strengthens the muscles, regulates internal organs functions.
Cooking time approx. 1 1/2 hours
Calories p. portion: 143
4 portions
Allergens: G

Quantity of ingredients:
Rice wild (nature rice) 1 cup / 100g. (recommended)
Water 8 cups / 900g. (yes)
Apple (sweet) 1 1/2 cups / 200g. (recommended)
Butter organic 1 table spoon / 10g. (yes)
Vanilla 1 pinch / 0,2g. (yes)
Sugar cane sugar 2 teaspoons / 6g. (little)

Cooking instructions:
Prepare rice congee according to basic recipe.

At the end, add finely chopped fruits to the season, vanilla, chili and butter; sweet to taste.

Variant: With nuts, the dish can always be made richer and more filling.

Effect: Cooked or steamed fruits are easier to digest and act better than raw. For some fruits, which are particularly suitable for hot summer days - such as melons and berries - it is still advisable to add the fruits only to a hot porridge.
Other types of fruit - such as apples, pears, plums and cherries - can also be simmered for a while.

9.64 Ribbon noodles with leaf spinach

Promotes digestion, improves blood circulation, forcing spleen and intestine, improves pancreatic function, Good to fight loss of appetite, flatulence, inflammatory bowel disease, obesity, stomach ulcers, stomach cramps, rheumatism, heartburn, twelffinger intestinal ulcers.
Cooking time approx. 45 min
Calories p. portion: 722
2 portions
Allergens: ACG

Quantity of ingredients:
Spinach 5/8 lbs - 8oz / 250g. (recommended)
Salt 1 pinch / 1g. (little)
Noodles (wheat, ribbon noodles) with egg 5/8 oz / 200g. (yes)
Olive oil 1 table spoon / 15g. (recommended)
Onion (spring onion) 1 piece / 20g. (yes)
Cream, sweet 30% 1/2 cup / 100g. (little)
Créme fraiche cheese 1/2 teaspoon / 6g. (yes)
Thyme dried 1/2 teaspoon / 2g. (yes)
Basil (fresh) 1/2 teaspoon / 2g. (yes)
Oregano dried 1/2 teaspoon / 2g. (yes)
Nutmeg 1 pinch / 0,5g. (yes)
Pepper (ground) 1 pinch / 0,5g. (yes)
Parmesan 1/2 oz / 20g. (yes)
Pine nuts 1 table spoon / 15g. (recommended)
Black caraway 1 pinch / 1g. (yes)

Cooking instructions:
Put the dripping wet spinach together with a little salt for 3 minutes ina pot, then drain in a sieve. Then finely cut.

Boil tagliatelle in plenty of salted water.

Heat the oil in a skillet and fry the spring onions rings. Add cream, crème fraiche, thyme, basil, oregano and nutmeg. Stir in the sauce while stirring. Add the spinach, heat briefly, season with nutmeg, salt and pepper.
Drain pasta and mix with the spinach. Season with salt and pepper. Portion noodles and serve with parmesan and pine nuts. Sprinkle the black cumin over it.

9.65 Rice congee with honey pear and black sesame

Promotes digestion, supports urination, good to fight blood circulation disorders, thromboses, risk of embolism, high blood pressure, a headache, heart attack and stroke.
Cooking time approx. 10 min - 3 hours
Calories p. portion: 158
2 portions
Allergens: N

Quantity of ingredients:
Basic recipe for a rice soup (Congee) 1 1/2 cups / 240g. (yes)
Pear 2 pieces / 300g. (recommended)
Sesame, black 1 teaspoon / 3g. (yes)

Cooking instructions:
Cook rice congee according to basic recipe.
Fill pot with 3 cm of water and heat till it boils. Quarter the pears (with the skin and seeds) and simmer them covered with black sesame for 10 minutes. Mix with the rice.

9.66 Rice with stewed vegetables

Reduces blood pressure, strengthens immune system, prevents cancer, reduces radiation damage, extremely low fat content, good to fight blood circulation disorders, thrombose, risk of embolism, a headache, heart attack and stroke. Is diuretic.
Cooking time approx. 20 min
Calories p. portion: 166
2 portions
Allergens: L

Quantity of ingredients:
Rice variety any 1/2 cup / 60g. (yes)
Water 3 cups / 300g. (yes)
Lemon peel 1 piece / 3g. (yes)
Water 1/2 cup / 0g. (yes)
Carrot 2 pieces / 180g. (recommended)
Celery sticks 1/2 piece / 5g. (yes)
Champignon 1/2 cup / 50g. (yes)
Cress 2 table spoons / 20g. (recommended)
Linseed oil 1 dash / 3g. (recommended)

Cooking instructions:
Cook rice according to basic recipe with a piece of lemon peel.
Steam chopped carrots, celery and mushrooms until soft.
Then sprinkle with cress. Then add a dash of high quality cold oil.

9.67 Roasted barley patties

Improves digestion, lowers cholesterol, good to fight diarrhea, ulceration, joint pain, stomach problems. Promotes spleen and liver, reduces blood pressure, strengthens immune system, prevents cancer, reduces radiation damage, stimulates liver function.
Cooking time approx. 1 1/2 hours
Calories p. portion: 398
3 portions
Allergens: ACN

Quantity of ingredients:
Water 1 1/2 cups / 250g. (yes)
Barley grouts 1 cup / 120g. (yes)
Potato 1 piece / 140g. (yes)

Carrot 1 piece / 120g. (recommended)
Champignon 2-3 pieces / 25g. (yes)
Chicken egg 1 piece / 55g. (little)
Onion white 1 piece / 50g. (yes)
Ginger fresh 1/2 teaspoon / 1g. (yes)
Pepper (ground) 1 pinch / 0,5g. (yes)
Salt 1 pinch / 1g. (little)
Lemon 1/2 piece / 15g. (yes)
Parsley 2 table spoons / 15g. (recommended)
Peppers powder 1 pinch / 1g. (yes)
Sesame oil 2 table spoons / 50g. (little)
Bread roll 1 piece / 35g. (yes)

Cooking instructions:
Preparation:
Place 2 large cups of hot water in a saucepan; add 1 large cup of barley porridge; simmer for 2 minutes while stirring; then let it swell for 20 minutes on the switched off stove; take down and let cool.

Cook in boiling water 1 large potato, chopped and cut.

Soak 1 roll in hot water and squeeze well.

Then: Mix the barley groats and crushed the potato. Add 1 grated carrot, 2 - 3 chopped mushrooms, 1 egg, 1 finely chopped onion, 1/2 teaspoon grated ginger, a pinch of pepper, a pinch of salt, a little lemon juice, chopped parsley, plenty of rose paprika; knead well and form patties; heat sesame oil in a hot pan; fry the patties for about 15 minutes over a gentle heat; turn at half time.

also fits well: lettuce, soybean vegetables.

9.68 Roasted nuts

Dissolves stones. Good to fight depressions. Strengths spleen and stomach.
Cooking time approx. 5 min
Calories p. portion: 973
2 portions
Allergens: H

Quantity of ingredients:
Hazelnuts   1/4 lbs - 4oz / 100g. (recommended)
Cashews   1/4 lbs - 4oz / 100g. (recommended)
Walnuts   1/4 lbs - 4oz / 100g. (yes)

Cooking instructions:
Roast nuts in a pan for about 5 minutes.

9.69 Semolina porridge with banana

Regulates gastrointestinal function, reduces inflammation, antiallergic, good to fight blood circulation disorders.
Cooking time approx. 15 min
Calories p. portion: 307
1 portions
Allergens: AG

Quantity of ingredients:
Cow's milk (whole milk 3.5% fat) 3/4 cup - 6 oz / 200g. (yes)
Spelled semolina 2 table spoons / 30g. (recommended)
Butter organic 1 teaspoon / 4g. (yes)
Banana 1/2 piece / 50g. (recommended)

Cooking instructions:
Heat the half of the milk in a small pot. Add the semolina and boil it shortly in the milk. Let it swell at low heat for 3 minutes with constant stirring. Remove the pot from the heat, add the remaining milk with the snow bean and place the mush in a small bowl. Add the butter and the battered banana.
For adults, a pinch of cinnamon can be spread over it.

9.70 Semolina soup with vegetables

Reduces blood pressure, strengthens immune system, prevents cancer, forcing spleen, dissolves stagnation, promotes weight loss. Good to fight immunodeficiency, loss of appetite, flatulence, high blood pressure, depressions, diabetes, diarrhea, rheumatism, heartburn, twelffinger intestinal ulcers.
Cooking time approx. 20 min
Calories p. portion: 105
3 portions
Allergens: AGL

Quantity of ingredients:
Basic recipe for a vegetable soup (nutritious) 2 cup / 500g.
(recommended)
Wheat semolina 2 table spoons / 20g. (yes)
Lovage 1/2 teaspoon / 2g. (yes)
Basil (fresh) 1/2 teaspoon / 1g. (yes)
Nutmeg 1 pinch / 0,1g. (yes)
Carrot 1/4 lbs - 4oz / 100g. (recommended)
Celery root 1/8 lbs - 2oz / 50g. (yes)
Cream, sweet 30% 2 table spoons / 30g. (little)
Parsley 1 table spoon / 10g. (recommended)

Cooking instructions:
Roast wheat grits without fat in a pan. Roast the chopped carrots and
celery briefly. Add the vegetable soup (Basic recipe for a vegetable
soup). Season with lovage, nutmeg and let it 10 min. simmer.
Stir in the cream before serving and garnish with parsley.

9.71 Spelled-grid porridge with berries of the season

Little laxative, strengthens immune system, activated cell metabolism,
reduces inflammation. Has a stabilizing effect on the blood circulation,
good to fight blood circulation disorders.
Cooking time approx. 15 min
Calories p. portion: 244
2 portions
Allergens: AGH

Quantity of ingredients:
Cow's milk (1.5% fat) 1/2 cup / 125g. (yes)
Water 1/2 cup / 125g. (yes)
Spelled semolina 5 table spoons / 50g. (recommended)
Butter organic 2 teaspoons / 20g. (yes)
Berries of the season 1/4 lbs - 4oz / 100g. (recommended)
Honey 1-2 teaspoons / 5g. (yes)
Almond 1-2 teaspoons / 5g. (recommended)
Peppermint 3-4 leaves / 2g. (yes)
Cinnamon ground 1 pinch / 0,5g. (yes)
Vanilla 1 pinch / 0,2g. (yes)
Cocoa 1 pinch / 0,5g. (yes)
Coconut grated 1 table spoon / 10g. (yes)

Cooking instructions:
Stir in spelled semolina in cold water and boil slowly over medium heat. After boiling, remove from the heat and let simmer for a few minutes. Depending on the desired consistency, some water may have to be added. Stir in the butter and fine grated nuts in the mash and raspberries. Serve with honey or whole-grain sugar as desired.
Spices and aromas: fresh mint, cinnamon or vanilla, cocoa, coconut

Summer: raspberries, blueberries, strawberries

9.72 Spicy avocado cream with cottage cheese

Anti-inflammatory, good to fight swelling, pain and itching, forcing spleen and digestive system, detoxifying, bactericide.
Cooking time approx. 15 min
Calories p. portion: 614
4 portions
Allergens: G

Quantity of ingredients:
Avocado 2 pieces / 600g. (recommended)
Pepper (ground) 1 pinch / 0,5g. (yes)
Salt 1 pinch / 1g. (little)
Lemon juice 1/2 piece / 15g. (yes)
Peppers powder 1 pinch / 1g. (yes)
Olive oil 1 table spoon / 10g. (recommended)
Herbs various 1 table spoon / 7g. (yes)
Cottage cheese 1 cup / 250g. (yes)
Bread with carob kernel flour 8 slices / 200g. (recommended)

Cooking instructions:
Peel, core and purée avocados; add plenty of ground pepper, salt, lemon juice, rose paprika, a few drops of oil, chili, fresh chopped herbs, a pinch of salt; cottage cheese (about the same amount as avocado cream), carefully submerge.

Goes well with: Potatoes and millet, with which the avocado cream in combination with vegetable dishes, legumes or lettuce leaves a delicious meal. It is also very good as an appetizer, as a souvenir at parties and as a morning meal in the summer together with a mild dish of lentils or Adzuki beans and grated radish.

9.73 Spicy Tofu Vegetable Pan

Forcing spleen, relieves constipation, detoxifying, reduces inflammation, improves blood circulation, promotes sweating, dissolves stagnation, reduces flatulence, reduces blood pressure, strengthens immune system, prevents cancer, reduces radiation damage.
Cooking time approx. 25 min
Calories p. portion: 241
4 portions
Allergens: EN

Quantity of ingredients:
Sesame oil 2 table spoons / 20g. (little)
Carrot 2 pieces / 100g. (recommended)
Fennel 1 piece / 250g. (recommended)
Leek 1 piece / 200g. (recommended)
Salt 1 pinch / 1g. (little)
Turmeric (yellow root) 1 pinch / 1g. (recommended)
Lemon juice 1 dash / 1g. (yes)
Soy Tofu 1 package / 120g. (recommended)
Pepper (ground) 1 pinch / 0,5g. (yes)
Soy sauce 1 dash / 3g. (yes)
Rice (whole grain) 1 cup / 120g. (recommended)
Water 6 cups / 500g. (yes)
Salt 1 pinch / 1g. (little)

Cooking instructions:
Heat sesame oil in a hot wok or a hot pan; fry the chopped carrots, fennel and leek slices; salt, a dash of lemon juice, turmeric, tofu cubes roast for 1 - 2 minutes.
Add the pepper and cook covered for about 5 minutes; drizzle with soy sauce. Place the rice in salted water, heat till it boils and let it simmer over low heat for about 15 minutes.

9.74 Spring salad

Blood-forming, blood detoxifying, diuretic, good to fight stomach discomfort, improves digestion, diarrhea, helps to digest fat, supports urination, reduces blood pressure, detoxifying, reduces inflammation, diuretic.
Cooking time approx. 10 min
Calories p. portion: 162
4 portions
Allergens: AEMN

Quantity of ingredients:
Sorrel 3/8 lbs - 6oz / 150g. (yes)
Dandelion (young plants) 1/4 lbs - 4oz / 100g. (yes)
Mung bean sprouting 0,2 lbs / 75g. (yes)
Cress 1/4 lbs - 4oz / 100g. (recommended)
Chives 1 Bunch / 50g. (recommended)
Tomato 2 pieces / 100g. (recommended)
Parsley 1 Bunch / 50g. (recommended)
Sesame paste (Tahini) 2 table spoons / 16g. (yes)
Soy sauce 1 dash / 3g. (yes)
Mustard 1/2 teaspoon / 2g. (recommended)
White bread (wheat bread) 6 slices / 120g. (little)

Cooking instructions:
Wash all salad´s, mix and prepare the sauce as follows:
Mix tahini with mustard and balsamic vinegar, tamari, olive oil, chives
and half of parsley. Pour the sauce over the salad and sprinkle the
remaining parsley just before serving.
Serve with the white bread.

9.75 Strawberry bananas mash

Regulates gastrointestinal function. Promotes digestion.
Cooking time approx. 10 min
Calories p. portion: 30
10 portions
Allergens:

Quantity of ingredients:
Banana 1 piece / 200g. (recommended)
Strawberries 5/8 oz / 200g. (yes)
Orange 1/2 piece / 70g. (recommended)

Cooking instructions:
Peel the banana. Wash the strawberries, pluck from the stems. Put both
in a mixing bowl. Add the orange juice and finely grate everything. Put
the marrow in an ice cube maker and freeze. Transfer the frozen cubes
to a cool box (shelf life of up to 2 months). Small portions are ideal for
mixing with yogurt or cottage cheese.

9.76 Supplementary nutrition

Protein-rich drink with very high energy density. Optimized protein content balances nitrogen losses and promotes protein anabolism.
Cooking time approx. 5 min
Calories p. portion: 1045
1 portions
Allergens:

Quantity of ingredients:
Supplementary nutrition 1 package / 250g. (yes)

Cooking instructions:
Use only as directed by the physician or therapist.

9.77 Sweet potato pancakes with basil pesto

Strengthens the immune system, reduces fat, Improves digestion, calms nerves and stomach, dissolves stones, improves blood circulation, strengthens the muscles, antioxidativ.
Cooking time approx. 30 min
Calories p. portion: 625
3 portions
Allergens: ACH

Quantity of ingredients:
Sweet potato 4 pieces / 500g. (yes)
Onion read 1/2 piece / 30g. (yes)
Basil 1 table spoon / 10g. (yes)
Chicken egg 2 pieces / 140g. (little)
Spelled wholemeal flour 3 oz / 80g. (recommended)
Salt 1 pinch / 0,5g. (little)
Olive oil 1/4 cup / 20g. (recommended)
Salt 1 teaspoon (coarse) / 3g. (little)
Basil Handful / 15g. (yes)
Parsley Handful / 15g. (recommended)
Garlic 2 cloves / 3g. (recommended)
Walnuts 1/8 lbs - 2oz / 60g. (yes)
Olive oil 2 table spoons / 20g. (recommended)

Cooking instructions:
Sweet Potato Buffer: Wash the sweet potato thoroughly, but do not peel, and grate into a large bowl. Add onion, basil, egg and flour, mix well and sprinkle with salt. The mixture can be formed into buffers. Bake

in a preheated tube on a baking tray coated with oil for 4 to 5 minutes on both sides.

Basil Pesto: Add the salt, chopped basil and parsley and crushed garlic in a small bowl and crush (if available, use the mortar). Add the grated walnuts. While stirring, add enough olive oil until the desired consistency is achieved.

9.78 Sweet rice with apples

Stops diarrhea, promotes digestion, appetizing, stops coughing, supports urination, many antioxidants. Little laxative.
Cooking time approx. 25 min
Calories p. portion: 156
4 portions
Allergens: H

Quantity of ingredients:
Rice sweet 1 cup / 100g. (yes)
Water 6 cups / 600g. (yes)
Apple juice (natural cloudy) 1 cup / 120g. (recommended)
Apple (sweet) 2 pieces / 300g. (recommended)
Apricot 2 pieces / 200g. (recommended)
Cinnamon ground 1 pinch / 0,3g. (yes)
Cardamom 1 pinch / 0,2g. (yes)
Ginger powder 1 knife tip / 0,3g. (yes)
Salt 1 pinch / 0,3g. (little)
Lemon 1/2 cut into pieces / 10g. (yes)
Cocoa 1 pinch / 0,5g. (yes)
Almond puree 2 table spoons / 20g. (yes)
Barley malt 1 table spoon / 10g. (yes)
Hazelnuts 2 table spoons / 20g. (recommended)

Cooking instructions:
Cook sweet rice in hot water.
Then: heat apple juice in a hot pot; chopped sweet apples, apricots or other sweet fruit (neutral or warm), cinnamon, cardamom, ginger, a pinch of salt, grated lemon peel, a little cocoa and simmer for a few minutes.

Stir in the boiled sweet rice, a little almond paste, some barley malt and heat; sprinkle with roasted nuts.

9.79 Szeged fishbowl

Promotes spleen, stomach and kidneys, improves digestion, dissolves stagnation, reduces blood pressure, strengthens immune system.
Cooking time approx. 30 min
Calories p. portion: 280
2 portions
Allergens: ADL

Quantity of ingredients:
Cod 5/8 oz / 200g. (recommended)
Lemon 1/4 piece / 5g. (yes)
Pork Bacon 1/8 lbs - 2oz / 40g. (little)
Onion (spring onion) 2 pieces / 40g. (yes)
Sauerkraut (cutted cabbage fermented) 5/8 lbs - 8oz / 250g. (yes)
Tomato paste 2 table spoons / 20g. (yes)
Basic recipe for a vegetable soup (nutritious) 1/2 cup / 150g. (recommended)
Salt 1 pinch / 1g. (little)
Peppers powder 1 pinch / 1g. (yes)
Ground caraway 1 pinch / 1g. (yes)
Pepper (ground) 1 pinch / 0,5g. (yes)
Spelled wholemeal flour 1 teaspoon / 3g. (recommended)
Bread with carob kernel flour 2 slices / 50g. (recommended)

Cooking instructions:
Clean the fish fillets, sprinkle with lemon, salt.
Roast the bacon in a deep, large pan. Add the finely chopped onions and roast for a short time. Add sauerkraut and tomato paste. Fill with vegetable stock and stew for about 10 to 15 minutes with the lid closed. Put prepared fish cubes on the sauerkraut. Season with paprika, caraway, pepper and simmer for about 10 minutes over low heat.
Tie with some flour or cornstarch.
Serve with bread.

9.80 Tea Green tea

Green tea promotes digestion, supports urination, dissolves mucus, detoxifying, stimulates nerves, reduces blood lipids, lowers cholesterol, reduces inflammation.
Cooking time approx. 10 min
Calories p. portion: 2
1 portions
Allergens:

Quantity of ingredients:
Green tea 1 teaspoon / 2g. (recommended)
Water 1 cup / 120g. (yes)

Cooking instructions:
For each cup you use a teaspoonful or a teabag.
Pour green tea only with 60 to 80 ° C / 140 to 176 °F hot water,
otherwise it will be bitter.
If the tea has a stimulating effect, let it draw for two to three minutes. It
has a calming effect for a duration of five minutes (no longer, otherwise
it will be bitter!).
Another method: Pour the tea leaves with about 70 ° C / 158 °F hot
water and pour the water immediately again. Then just pour hot water
again. The bitter substances disappear and the tea gets a milder
aroma.

9.81 Tomato soup

Promotes digestion, helps to digest fat, supports urination, reduces
blood pressure, dissolves stagnation. Contains unsaturated fatty acids,
is antioxidativ.
Cooking time approx. 10 min
Calories p. portion: 100
2 portions
Allergens:

Quantity of ingredients:
Olive oil 1 table spoon / 15g. (recommended)
Onion white 1 piece / 60g. (yes)
Cinnamon ground 1 pinch / 1g. (yes)
Basil (fresh) 1 teaspoon / 2g. (yes)
Pepper (ground) 1 pinch / 0,5g. (yes)
Salt 1 pinch / 1g. (little)
Tomato 6 pieces / 250g. (recommended)
Peppers powder 1 pinch / 1g. (yes)
Water 5/8 lbs - 8oz / 250g. (yes)

Cooking instructions:
Roast the onion in a pot. Salt and spices. Briefly roast. Put washed and
quartered tomatoes in the pan. Stir and sauté briefly. Add a quart of
water and heat till it boils. Cook for a quarter of an hour and puree.

9.82 Tsampa

Promotes spleen, diuretic, forcing spleen, supports urination, relaxes.
Promotes digestion, detoxifying, stimulates nerves, reduces blood
lipids, lowers cholesterol.
Cooking time approx. 5 min
Calories p. portion: 140
2 portions
Allergens: A

Quantity of ingredients:
Tsampa (roasted barley flour) 4 table spoons / 30g. (yes)
Green tea 1 cup / 120g. (recommended)
Water 1 cup / 120g. (yes)

Cooking instructions:
Tsampa is traditionally made with tea.
The tsampa is poured into a bowl and doused with tea, part of which is
drunk and the remainder made into a dough-like mass with tsampa.
You can also pour the tea first; In any case, it takes some skill to
achieve the right balance of tsampa and liquid. The two substances are
usually mixed with your fingers. It is recommended to add yak butter to
improve taste and stability.

9.83 Vegetable bowl with Provencal pistou

Promotes spleen and liver, reduces blood pressure, strengthens
immune system, prevents cancer, reduces radiation damage, forcing
spleen, dissolves stagnation. Relieves constipation, strengthens mother
milk production.
Cooking time approx. 1 1/2 hours
Calories p. portion: 138
8 portions
Allergens: AGL

Quantity of ingredients:
Tomato 5/8 oz / 200g. (recommended)
Olive oil 2 table spoons / 30g. (recommended)
Garlic 1 clove / 5g. (recommended)
Toast bread (whole grain) 1 slice / 5g. (yes)
Parmesan 1 oz / 30g. (yes)
Basil (fresh) 1 Bunch / 125g. (yes)
Salt 1 pinch / 2g. (little)
Pepper (ground) 1 pinch / 1g. (yes)

Oregano dried 1 teaspoon / 3g. (yes)
Basic recipe for a vegetable soup (nutritious) 3 lbs / 1250g. (recommended)
Carrot 3/8 lbs - 6oz / 150g. (recommended)
Celery root 1/4 lbs - 4oz / 100g. (yes)
Broccoli 5/8 oz / 200g. (recommended)
Fennel 1 piece / 250g. (recommended)
Thyme dried 1/2 teaspoon / 2g. (yes)
Oregano dried 1/2 teaspoon / 2g. (yes)
Bay leaf 1 piece / 0,5g. (yes)
Peas, green 1/8 lbs - 2oz / 50g. (yes)
Onion (spring onion) 4 pieces / 80g. (yes)
Potato 1/4 lbs - 4oz / 100g. (yes)

Cooking instructions:
Sauce:
Tear off tomatoes and cut into small pieces. Reduce in a pot with a little oliv oil, finely chopped garlic. Add 1 slice of dry toasted bread (crumbed), fresh finely grated Parmesan, finely chopped basil, oregano, salt and pepper.

Soup:
Boil the vegetable broth according to the basic recipe, add coarsely sliced carrots, diced celery, diced potatoes, small florets, broccoli, finely chopped fennel tuber, peas, thyme, oregano and the bay leaf. let cook 10 minutes.

Cut 4 scallions into thin rings, add them and cook another 2 min.

Pour sauce into a soup bowl. First only a few tablespoons. Stir boiling broth with it, then stir in the soup little by little.

9.84 Vegetable juice

Promotes digestion, helps to digest fat, supports urination, reduces blood pressure, strengthens immune system, prevents cancer, reduces radiation damage, forcing spleen, is stimulating.
Cooking time approx. 15 min
Calories p. portion: 64
1 portions
Allergens: L

Quantity of ingredients:
Celery root 1/2 oz / 20g. (yes)
Carrot 1/4 lbs - 4oz / 100g. (recommended)
Tomato 1/4 lbs - 4oz / 100g. (recommended)
Garlic 1 piece / 2g. (recommended)
Salt 1 teaspoon / 2g. (little)
Acerola fruit nectar or powder 1/2 teaspoon / 1g. (recommended)

Cooking instructions:
Peel all ingredients and use the juicer to make a drink. Stir in the acerola.

9.85 Vegetable miso soup with tofu

Very powerful, strengthens after febrile illness, reduces blood pressure, strengthens immune system, prevents cancer, reduces radiation damage, improves blood circulation, strengthens liver and kidney, detoxifying, strengthens the muscles, reduces flatulence, forcing spleen.
Cooking time approx. 15 min
Calories p. portion: 107
4 portions
Allergens: EN

Quantity of ingredients:
Sesame oil 2 table spoons / 35g. (little)
Onion (shallot) 1 piece / 20g. (yes)
Carrot 1 piece / 70g. (recommended)
Leek 2 inches / 10g. (recommended)
Water 3 cups / 750g. (yes)
Endive salad 2 table spoons / 30g. (yes)
Soy Tofu 2 table spoons / 30g. (recommended)
Ginger fresh 1/2 teaspoon / 1g. (yes)
Miso 2 table spoons / 15g. (yes)

Cooking instructions:
In sesame oil first sauté onions, then carrots and a little leek; Pour in water and simmer gently; add the bean sprouts and endive leaves and leave to stand; Tofu cubes, add a little ginger; at the end stir in a little cooled cooking-water the Miso.

9.86 Warming carrot soup

Strengthens and warms, reduces blood pressure, strengthens immune system, prevents cancer, reduces radiation damage, strengthens gastrointestinal function.
Cooking time approx. 30 min
Calories p. portion: 133
3 portions
Allergens: HL

Quantity of ingredients:
Carrot 4 pieces / 250g. (recommended)
Walnut oil 2 table spoons / 20g. (little)
Onion (shallot) 2 pieces / 40g. (yes)
Anise (Common Fennel) 1/2 teaspoon / 1g. (yes)
Nutmeg 1 pinch / 1g. (yes)
Ginger fresh 1/2 teaspoon / 1g. (yes)
Salt 1 pinch / 1g. (little)
Basic recipe for a vegetable soup (nutritious) 2 cup / 500g. (recommended)
Parsley 1 table spoon / 10g. (recommended)

Cooking instructions:
Heat walnut oil in a hot pot and fry onions; steam the carrots in it; add anise, nutmeg, a little ginger, salt and sauté everything; add water or vegetable- or meat stock; cook everything soft and then puree; fold in parsley at the end.

Recommendation: Suitable for the cold season, especially if you use meat broth as a liquid for infusion.

9.87 Yellow lentil soup

Strengthens heart and kidney, diuretic, promotes spleen, calms the stomach, promotes digestion, strengthens immune system, prevents cancer, reduces radiation damage, stimulates liver function, antioxidativ.
Cooking time approx. 20 min
Calories p. portion: 155
7 portions
Allergens: A

Quantity of ingredients:
Lentils yellow 1 lbs / 500g. (yes)
Carrot 2 pieces / 150g. (recommended)
Kohlrabi 1 piece / 300g. (recommended)
Onion white 1 piece / 50g. (yes)
Parsley 1/2 bunch / 100g. (recommended)
Turmeric (yellow root) 1 pinch / 1g. (recommended)
Cardamom 1 pinch / 1g. (yes)
Salt 1 pinch / 1g. (little)
Olive oil 1 table spoon / 10g. (recommended)
Water 4 cup / 1000g. (yes)
Lemon juice 1/2 piece / 15g. (yes)
White bread (wheat bread) 7 slices / 140g. (little)

Cooking instructions:
Wash lenses well in a colander. Heat oil in a pot. Add finely chopped
onion, sliced carrots, diced kohlrabi and spices, sauté and salt. Add the
lentils and cover with water and simmer for 20 minutes. Add water as
needed and season with salt. Sprinkle with fresh parsley or fresh green
cilantro and drizzle with lemon juice.
Here you can also use red lenses. (same cooking time).
Serve with white bread.

9.88 Zucchini with basil pesto

Good to fight bloating and nausea. Relaxing and reassuring, promotes
digestion, forcing spleen and digestive system, detoxifying, strengthens
the muscles and bones, diuretic, supports urination, dissolves
stagnation.
Cooking time approx. 25 min
Calories p. portion: 468
3 portions
Allergens: ACGHL

Quantity of ingredients:
Basil (fresh) 1 Bunch / 125g. (yes)
Olive oil 1 table spoon / 20g. (recommended)
Almond 1 table spoon / 15g. (recommended)
Parmesan 1 oz / 30g. (yes)
Basic recipe for a vegetable soup (nutritious) 2 table spoons / 45g.
(recommended)
Lemon peel 1 teaspoon / 3g. (yes)
Lemon 1 teaspoon / 3g. (yes)

Oregano dried 2 teaspoons / 15g. (yes)
Ground 1 pinch / 1g. (yes)
Salt 1 pinch / 1g. (little)
Pepper (ground) 1 pinch / 1g. (yes)
Noodles (wheat, spaghetti) with egg 5/8 oz / 200g. (yes)
Salt 1 pinch / 1g. (little)
Olive oil 1 table spoon / 15g. (recommended)
Onion (spring onion) 2 pieces / 40g. (yes)
Zucchini 5/8 lbs - 8oz / 250g. (yes)

Cooking instructions:
Mix Basil, olive oil, grated almonds, parmesan, vegetable broth and grated lemon peel to a smooth cream puree. Season the pesto with salt, oregano, cumin and pepper.

Boil the spaghetti with a little salt in plenty of water.

Heat the olive oil in a pan and fry the spring onions while stirring. Add zucchini and fry briefly with stirring. The zucchini should be soft with a bite. Season the zucchini with salt.

In a bowl, mix well-drained spaghetti with zucchini and pesto. Season the spaghetti with salt and pepper.

Recommended for dysphagia, loss of appetite, potassium and magnesium requirements.

10 Effects of food

10.1 Use ingredients: recommendable

Acai powder
Acerola fruit nectar or powder
Almond
Apple (sour)
Apple (sweet)
Apple juice (natural cloudy)
Apple puree
Apricot
Apricot nectar
Apricots
Apricots juice
Avocado
Banana
Banana (cooking banana)
Barley flour
Barley not peeled
Basic recipe for a fish soup
Basic recipe for a vegetable soup
(nutritious)
Berries of the season
Berry juice
Bitter Herb liqueur
Blueberry
Blueberry juice
Brazil nuts
Bread with carob kernel flour
Broccoli
Buckwheat
Buckwheat (roasted) Kasha
Buckwheat whole grain
Bulgur (cereals)
Cantaloupe
Carrot
Carrot (Early Carrot)
Carrot juice without sugar
Cashews
Cherry juice
Chestnut puree
Chestnuts
Chives
Cod
Codfish
Compote (fruits of the season)
Couscous
Cranberries
Cranberry
Cranberry
Cranberry juice
Cream 10% coffee cream

Cress
Currant (black)
Currant jam (black)
Currant juice (black)
Fennel
Fish pieces mixed (fresh water)
Flounder
Fox nut, gorgon nut, makhana
Fruit mix juice
Garlic
Gooseberry
Grape juice red
Grape juice white
Grapes white
Green spelt
Green tea
Halibut (Flatfish)
Hazelnuts
Hibiscus
Kiwi
Kohlrabi
Kudzu
Lamb's lettuce
Leek
Lemon Balm (fresh)
Lettuce
Lily bulbs
Linseed
Linseed (crushed)
Linseed oil
Mango juice
Manioc flour
Maple syrup
Mediterranean fish (cod, plaice,
haddock, sea eel, mackerel)
Millet flakes
Mullet
Mustard
Mustard medium hot
Mustard seeds
Mustard sweet
Oat fusion (baby food)
Olive oil
Orange
Orange juice
Parsley
Peanut oil
Peanuts
Pear

Pear juice
Pearl barley
Peppers
Pine nuts
Pistachios
Plaice
Radish
Radish (white, green, purple-red)
Radish black
Radish horseradish
Rice (whole grain)
Rice wild (nature rice)
Rosefish
Rucola
Rye wholemeal bread
Savory
Sea buckthorn
Soy flour
Soy noodles
Soy Tofu
Soya Cuisine (soy cream)
Soybeans

Soybeans, yellow
Spelled (Dark) bread
Spelled flakes
Spelled grain
Spelled semolina
Spelled wholemeal flour
Spinach
Tomato
Tomato juice
Tuna
Turmeric (yellow root)
Vegetable juice
Walnuts roasted
Wheat bran
Wheat bulgur
Wheat flour whole grain
Wheat semolina for children
Wheat/Rye/Gray-black bread with yeast
White cabbage
Whole grain bread
Wholemeal flour
Wild strawberries

10.2 Use ingredients: yes

Adzuki beans
Agar agar (kelp)
Agave nectar
Agrimony
Almond marzipan
Almond milk
Almond puree
Aloe juice
Amaranth
Amaranth Pops
Anchovy / Sardine
Angelica root
Anise (Common Fennel)
Apricot dried
Apricot jam
Arrowroot
Artichoke
Asparagus (green or white)
Aubergine
Baking powder
Balm
Bamboo shoots
Banchatee (green tea)
barberry
Barley
Barley grass powder
Barley grouts
Barley malt
Basic recipe for a beef soup

Basic recipe for a rice soup (Congee)
Basil
Basil (fresh)
Batavia
Bay leaf
Beans (green, fresh)
Bearberry leaf
Beef fillet
Beef meat
Beef meat (calf)
Beer (alcohol-free)
Beer (alcohol-reduced)
Bitter Lemon
Bitter orange peel
Black beans
Black caraway
Black fungus mushroom
Black tea
Blackberry dried (unripe fruit)
Blackberry jam
Blackberry leaves
Blackberry´s
Black-eyed peas
Blackthorn (Sloe)
Blue mallow tee
Blueberry dried
Blueberry jam
Bocksdorn fruits (Fructus Lycii, Goji,
goji berry dried

Boletus mushroom
Borage
Boxhorn clover seeds
Bread roll
Breadcrumbs (wheat bread, bread roll)
Brie cheese
Broad beans (thick beans)
Brussels sprouts
Buckbean
Burdock root tea
Bush beans
Butter (half fat)
Butter beans white
Butter organic
Buttermilk
Calamari
Camembert
Capers in olive oil
Carambola (Star fruit)
Cardamom
Carob flour, St. john's bread
Carp
Cauliflower
Caviar
Celery root
Celery sticks
Cereal coffee
Chamomile
Chamomile tea
Champignon
Channa-Dal
Chanterelle
Chard
Chenpi (chinese tangerine bowl)
Cherry
Cherry (sour)
Cherry compote
Chervil
Chervil dried
Chickpeas
Chickweed
Chicory
Chili (pod or ground)
Chinese cabbage
Chinese pearl barley
Chlorella (fresh water)
Chrysanthemum blossom tea
Cinnamon ground
Cinnamon sticks
Clementine
Clementines
Clove
Cocoa
Coconut flakes

Coconut grated
Coconut meat
Coconut milk
Coffee
Coix (seeds) YiYi Ren
Cola drink
Coriander
Coriander (fresh)
Corn
Corn (fast polenta)
Corn (roasted)
Corn flour
Corn Grease (Polenta)
Corn silk tea
Corn starch
Cottage cheese
Cow's milk (1.5% fat)
Cow's milk (whole milk 3.5% fat)
Crab
Cranberry jam
Cream sour 10%
Creamer
Créme fraiche cheese
Crispbread
Crucian
Cucumber
Cucumber (bitter)
Cucumber (spicy cucumber)
Cumin (Caraway seed)
Curcuma
Curd cheese 20%
Currant (red)
Currant (white)
Currant jam (red)
Currants (black)
Currants (red)
Curry
Curry paste red
Daisy
Dandelion (young plants)
Dandelion juice
Dandelionroots tea
Dashi
Dates dried
Dates red
Deer meat
Deer meat
Deer's Bones
Deer's kidneys
Dill
Duck (heart)
Dulse (seawood)
Dyer's broom herb
Edam cheese

Eel
Elderberries
Elderberry blossom tee
Emmental cheese
Endive salad
Fennel seeds ground
Fennel tea
Fenugreek (Trigonella foenum-graecum)
Feta cheese
Feta cheese
Fig
Fig dried
Fish innards
Fish remains
Fish sauce
Flower pollen
French beans
Fresh cheese
Fresh cheese from soya
Fresh cheese with herbs
Freshwater crab
Freshwater fish
Fructose (glucose)
Fruit tea
Gail plum
Galangal
Garam Masala powder
Gelatin white
Gelee Royal
Gentian root
Gentian root tea
Ginger fresh
Ginger powder
Ginkgo fruit
Ginseng
Ginseng root
Goat and sheep's milk
Goat cheese
Goose blood
Gorgonzola
Gouda cheese
Gourd
Grapefruit (Pomelo)
Grapefruit dried peel
Grapefruit juice
Grapes red
Grass carp
Greengage
Ground

Ground caraway
Guava
Hawthorn

Herbal tea mix
Herbs bitter
Herbs of Provence
Herbs various
Herbs wild
Herring
Hibiscus tea
Hijiki
Hokkaido pumpkin
Honey
Hop
Horehound leaves
Horse meat
Hyssop
Iceberg lettuce
Jasmine blossoms tee
Jellyfish
Juniper berry
Kaki plum
Kalmus
Kefir
Kidney beans (red)
King Solomon's-seal
Kombu seaweed (Saccharina japonica)
Kukicha tea
Kumquats
Ladyfingers
Lamb's lettuce
Lavender blossoms
Leaf salads (bitter)
Lemon
Lemon Balm (dried)
Lemon juice
Lemon peel
Lemongrass
Lentils
Lentils black
Lentils red
Lentils yellow
Licorice root tea
Lima beans
Lime
Lime blossom tea
Liver smoothing tea
Longane
Loquate / Japanese medlar
Lotus roots
Lotus seeds
Lovage
Lovage seeds
Luo Han Guo fruit
Lychee
Lychee in Preserved
Lye roll

Mackerel
Mallow (Malva sylvestris) blossom tea
Malt
Mango
Mare's milk
Marjoram
Medlar
Mineral water
Mirabelle plum
Miso
Miso black (fermented)
Miso paste (soy bean paste)
Mixed Pickles
Mold cheese
Morel (black, dried)
Morel, dried
Mozzarella
Mu Erh Mushroom
Muesli
Mulberry fruit
Mulled Wine Spice
Multi-grain bread (gray bread)
Mung bean
Mung bean sprouting
Mussels
Mustard Dijon
Mutton
Nasturtium (nose-twister or nose-tweaker)
Nectarine
Nettles
Noodles (wheat) with egg
Noodles (wheat, lasagne) with egg
Noodles (wheat, ribbon noodles) with egg
Noodles (wheat, spaghetti) with egg
Noodles (whole grain) with egg
Nori, purple seaweed, red algae
Nutmeg
Oat
Oat flakes (whole grain)
Oat flakes roasted
Oat flour
Oat meal
Oat milk
Octopus
Octopus
Okra
Olives
Olives green
Onion (shallot)
Onion (spring onion)
Onion read
Onion white

Orange blossom
Orange dried peel
Orange grated peel
Orange jam
Orange peel
Oregano dried
Oregano fresh
Oyster mushroom
Oyster shell powder
Oysters
Palm oil
Papaya
Parmesan
Parsley root
Parsnip
Passion blossoms tea
Passion fruit
Peaches
Peaches (canned)
Peanut butter
Pearl barley
Peas
Peas, green
Pepper (ground)
Pepper Cayenne
Pepper powder (hot)
Pepper white (ground)
Peppercorns
Peppermint
Peppermint tea
Pepperoni
Pepperoni, red, pitted, halved
Pepperoni, yellow, pitted, halved
Peppers (rose peppers)
Peppers (sweet)
Peppers powder
Perch
Pheasant
Pickle
Pigeon
Pigeon egg
Pimento
Pineapple
Pineapple juice without sugar
Pinto beans speckled
Plum
Plum dried
Plums
Pomegranate
Poppy
Potato
Potato (mealy)
Potato flour
Prickly pear

Processed cheese 12%
Psyllium seed
Pudding powder vanilla
Puff pastry
Pumpernickel (dark bread)
Pumpkin
Pumpkin seeds
Quince
Quinoa
Rabbit
Rabbit (wild)
Rabbit meat
Radicchio
Radish leaves
Raisins
Raspberry
Raspberry dried (immature)
Raspberry jam
Raspberry leaf tea
Red beet
Red berry (without sugar)
Red cabbage
Reishi mushroom
Rhubarb
Ribworttea
Rice (fragrance)
Rice (Gaoliang / Sorghum)
Rice Basmati
Rice black
Rice flour
Rice long grain rice
Rice malt
Rice mash
Rice noodles
Rice red
Rice round grain
Rice starch
Rice sticky
Rice sweet
Rice variety any
Romaine lettuce / lettuce salad
Rose blossom tea
Rose hip
Rose hip tea
Rose leaf tea
Rosemary
Rusk
Rye
Rye flour
Safflower (Dyer's thistle / Hong Hua)
Saffron
Sage
Sago (cereals)
Sake

Salmon
Salsify
Sauerkraut (cutted cabbage fermented)
Savoy cabbage / kale
Sea cucumber
Seacrab
Sesame paste (Tahini)
Sesame, black
Sesame, white
Shark
Sheep's milk
Sheep's milk yoghurt
Shiitake, dried
Shrimp
Shrimps
Skim milk powder
Slug
Sorrel
Sour cherries
Sour cream 15% fat
Sour milk
Sour milk cheese 20%
Sourdough
Soy sauce
Soybean milk
Soybeans, black
Soybeans, blacks, fermented
Spiny lobsters
Spurdog (spiny dogfish, Schillerlocken)
St. Benedict's thistle, blessed thistle,
holy thistle, spotted thistle
Star anise
Stevia (candyleaf, sweetleaf)
Strawberries
Strawberry jam
Strawberry Juice
Sugar fructose - fruit sugar
Sugar glucose - grapes sugar
Sugar Milk Sugar
Sugar substitute (sweetener)
Sunflower seeds
Supplementary nutrition
Sweet potato
Tabasco
Tangerine
Tarragon (Estragon)
Tea mixture uric acid lowering
Thyme
Thyme dried
Toast bread (whole grain)
Tomato dried
Tomato paste
Tomato puree
Tonic Water

Topinambur
Trout
Trout (smoked)
Truffle
Tsampa (roasted barley flour)
Turkey breast meat
Turkey ham
Turnip
Turnips
Umeboshi paste
Umeboshi plums (Japanese apricots)
Valerian
Vanilla
Vanilla pod
Vanilla powder
Vanilla sugar natural
Vinegar (Apple vinegar)
Vinegar (Red wine vinegar)
Vinegar Aceto Balsamico
Vinegar Aceto Balsamico white
Wakame
Walnuts
Water
Water hot
Watermelon

Wax gourd
Wheat
Wheat flakes
Wheat flour
Wheat semolina
Wheatgrass juice
Wheatgrass powder
Whey
White beans
Whitefish
Wild boar meat
Wild garlic (garlic spinach)
Wild herbs
Wormwood
Wormwood herb
Yam root, yam root tuber
Yarrow
Yarrow tea
Yeast
Yew nut
Yoghurt vanilla
Yogi tea
Yogurt (natural, 1.5% fat)
Yogurt (natural, 3.5% fat)
Zucchini

10.3 Use ingredients: little

Bean oil
Beef heart
Beef heart (calf)
Beef kidney
Beef liver
Beef lungs (calf)
Beef meatbones
Beef Oxtail pieces
Beef soup meat
Beef stomach
Beer (Pils)
Beer (Top-fermented German dark beer)
Bitter liqueur
Borage oil
Brown ale
Campari
Chicken Blood
Chicken egg
Chicken egg white
Chicken heart
Chicken liver
Chicken meat
Chicken stomach
Chicken yolk

Chocolate
Chocolate (Diabetic)
Coconut fat
Cola drink (low calorie)
Corn germ oil
Cream (30% fat)
Cream sour 20%
Cream sour 30%
Cream, sweet 30%
Curd cheese 40%
Eel smoked
Evening primrose oil
Fernet Branca (herbal bitter liqueur)
Ginger oil
Ginseng liqueur
Goat and sheep's blood
Goat and sheep's brain
Goat and sheep's liver
Goat and sheep's stomach
Goose parts
Grapeseed oil
Honey wine (Met)
Lamb bones
Lamb kidneys
Lamb liver

Lamb meat
Lobster
Lychee liqueur
Margarine
Margarine (diet)
Martini
Mascarpone cheese
Mayonnaise 50%
Mayonnaise 80%
Millet
Mutton
Peanut (roasted)
Pig blood
Pineapple (from a can)
Pork Bacon
Pork brain
Pork ham
Pork ham cooked
Pork ham smoked
Pork heart
Pork kidneys
Pork liver
Pork lung
Pork marrow bones
Pork meat
Pork skin
Pork stomach
Pork's intestine
processed cheese 30%
Prosecco
Pumpkin seed oil
Quail egg

Rabbit liver
Red wine
Rum
Salt
Salt (herbal)
Sesame oil
Sesame oil roasted
Sherry (whine)
Soy Tofu smoked
Soybean oil
Spirit
Sugar - icing sugar
Sugar brown
Sugar candy white
Sugar cane sugar
Sugar molasses
Sugar palm sugar
Sugar white
Sunflower oil
Thistle oil
Walnut oil
Wheat beer
Wheat flatbread/pita bread
Wheat germ oil
White bread (baguette)
White bread (pretzel sticks)
White bread (roll)
White bread (wheat bread)
White breadcrumbs
White dumpling bread (wheat bread cut into chunks)
White wine

10.4 Do not use contra-acting foods

Beef bone marrow
Clarified butter
Cooking oil
Duck (slaughtered)
Ducks egg
Goat
Goose
Goose egg
Goose fat

Lamb shoulder
Pork fat (lard)
Pork knuckle
Pork Lard
Pork sausage (Bratwurst) Pork/beef sausage (smoked)
Quail
Rapeseed oil

11 Herbs and their effects

11.1 Basil

It has a beneficial effect on flatulence and nausea, relaxing and soothing. Good to fight emphysema, bronchitis, whooping cough, high blood pressure, headache, mouth odor, warts, hiccup, gout, migraine.

11.2 Nettles

Promotes urination. Tea or juice, cleanses the blood and the kidneys, supports prostate problems, inhibit the formation of inflammation, pain-relieving.

11.3 Dill

The medicinal and spice herb has an antispasmodic effect and stimulates gastric juice production. Good to fight flatulence. Antispasmodic for gastrointestinal discomfort.

11.4 Chervil dried

Forces urination, detoxifying, blood-purifying and blood-pressure-reducing effects.

11.5 Coriander

The essential oils are appetizing, digestive, cramping and soothing in stomach and intestinal disorders.

11.6 Herbs various

Appetizing, lots of trace elements and vitamins

11.7 Cress

Diuretic, supports urination. Good to fight dry mouth, inner agitation, sore throat, diabetes, kidney stones, gastrointestinal complaints, lung problems, menstrual cramps or cancer.

11.8 Chives

Bactericide, prevents cancer, strengthens gastric juice production, promotes digestion and blood circulation, promotes growth, triggers stagnation.

11.9 Lovage

Stimulates digestion, reduces pain. Extracts of the root are used to flush out urinary tract infections and prevent kidney gravel.

11.10 Lily bulbs

Calms nerves, good to fight scaly skin. The onions and the petals are added to ointments in the Orient, which can heal muscles and tendons. White lily (astringent).

11.11 Dandelion (young plants)

Detoxifies, relieves inflammation. Regulates digestion, helps with rheumatism, releases kidney stones, leaves pimples and chronic skin disorders disappear.

11.12 Marjoram

Helps to digest fat foods, strengthens digestive organs, helps to fight colds, strengthens menstruation, promotes skin healing.

11.13 Oregano dried

It has an anti-digestive, calming and nerve-strengthening effect, helps to fight cramping stomach and intestinal disorders. The ingredient Carvacrol has an anti-inflammatory effect.

11.14 Parsley

Stimulates liver function, detoxifies. Forces urinating. Relieves flatulence. Digestive and menstrual stimulating, birth-accelerating, memory-enhancing, blood-purifying, skin-smoothing.

11.15 Peppermint

Relaxes, frees the lungs and the nose (inhale), regulates the cycle. Stimulates bile flow and bile production, antispasmodic in gastrointestinal disorders, antimicrobial and antiviral.

11.16 Rosemary

Promotes digestion, relieves bloating, strengthens lung, spleen and kidney. Affects the circulation and nerves. Appetizing. Baths help to fight circulatory disorders as well as with gout and rheumatism.

11.17 Sage

Good to fight yeast infections. The leaves have a digestive effect and are used in greasy foods. Antiperspirant effect. Helps to relieve coughing attacks. Dries out (TCM).

11.18 Sorrel

Astringent, hematopoietic, purifies the blood, diuretic. Good to fight liver weakness, upset stomach, indigestion, constipation, diarrhea, worms, scurvy, anemia, women's complaints, wounds, skin rashes, boils, ulcers, swelling.

11.19 Black caraway

Detoxifying, immunoregulatory. In addition, the oil should stimulate the formation of bone marrow cells and generally protect body cells from viruses.

11.20 Thyme dried

Disinfecting. It stimulates the blood circulation, increases the appetite and helps to digest fat meat better. Strengthens lungs and spleen (TCM).

11.21 King Solomon's-seal

Used to repair wounds or damaged tissue. Good to fight dry cough, earlier also tuberculosis and dysentery, as well as diarrhea and hemorrhoids.

11.22 Yam root, yam root tuber

Solves cramps (in the gastrointestinal tract). Digestive through increased bile production. Anti-inflammatory in rheumatic diseases. Mucolytic agent for coughing. Relief of menopausal symptoms.

11.23 Lemon Balm (fresh)

Stimulating, antibacterial, encouraging, relaxing, antispasmodic, cooling, antipyretic, analgesic, sweat-inducing, virus-inhibiting. Good for colds, fever, flu, cough, bronchitis, asthma, loss of appetite, bloating, heartburn.

12 Basics of Nutrition

The basic principles of nutrition described herein are general recommendations. They are not aimed at a specific form of therapy. Recommendations concerning a therapy have priority.

12.1 Nutrition

Regular meals in a relaxed atmosphere. A warm breakfast is considered a good start into the day.
The main meals ought to be taken for lunch – supper in the early evening. Pay attention to feeling hungry or sated: don't eat too much nor remain hungry is the rule
Prepare the meals freshly from natural, regional products. Frozen, heat-conserved, industrially prepared or foodstuffs cooked in the microwave oven are rejected.
Choice of foodstuffs according to the season: more cooling food in summer, more warming food in winter.
Eat cooked food at least twice a day. Food and drinks ought to be lukewarm, never ice-cold or hot.
Raw vegetables, briefly cooked vegetables, freshly squeezed juices and mineral water are not recommended. Milk and dairy products are only included in the diet if they don't cause problems.
Don't use therapeutic recipes over a longer period without consulting your doctor or therapist.

Varied food
Enjoy the diversity of foodstuffs. Characteristics of a balanced nutrition are variety, suitable combination and a balanced quantity of rich and low energy foodstuffs (on one hand avoiding undersupply with essential nutrients and on the other hand to take to many undesirable substances).

A lot of Cereal Products - and Potatoes
Bread, pasta, rice, cereal flakes (best wholemeal) as well as potatoes contain almost no fat, but many vitamins, mineral nutrients, trace elements, roughage and secondary plant substances. These foodstuffs ought to be taken with low-fat side dishes.

Vegetables and Fruit – „Take Five" every day ...
5 portions of vegetables and fruit a day, as fresh as possible, briefly cooked, or maybe one portion as a juice – ideal as a side dish to every meal as well as snack between meals: Thus a lot of vitamins, mineral nutrients as well as roughage and secondary plant substances

Daily milk and dairy products

Milk and Dairy Products every Day, once or twice per Week Fish; meat, sausages as well as eggs moderately. These foodstuffs contain valuable nutrients like calcium in the milk, iodine selenium and omega-3 fat acids in saltwater fish. Meat is favorable due to its high content of disposable iron and the vitamins B1, B6 and B12. Quantities of 300 – 600 g meat and sausage per week are sufficient. Prefer low-fat products, especially in meat- and dairy products.

Low-fat and fatty Foodstuffs

Fat supplies us with essential fat acids and fatty foodstuffs contain also fat-soluble vitamins. Fat is high in energy; therefore much fat in the food may cause overweight, possibly also cancer. Too many saturated fat acids may further a tendency for cardio-vascular diseases in the long term. Prefer vegetable oils and fats (e.g. rapeseed-, olive-, soya-oils and solid fats produced therefrom). Beware of invisible fat in meat- and dairy products, pastry and sweets as well as in fast-food and convenience foods. 70 – 90 g fat per day is sufficient.

Moderately Sugar and Salt

Take sugar and foods/drinks containing various kinds of sugar (e.g. glucose syrup) only occasionally. Use herbs and spices as well as a little salt creatively. Prefer salt containing iodine.

Plenty of Liquids

Water is absolutely essential. Drink 1-2 l liquids every day. Prefer water (with or without gas) and other low-calorie drinks. Alcoholic drinks should not be taken.

Tasty Dishes, carefully cooked

Cook the meals with as low temperatures and as short as possible, using little water and fat – this preserves the original taste, keeps the nutrients intact and prevents the production of harmful compounds.

Take time and enjoy the food

Take your Time and enjoy your Food
Eating consciously helps to eat right. The eye enjoys food, too. It's fun, invites to enjoy varied dishes and stimulates the feeling of satiety.

Watch your Weight and stay in Motion

A balanced diet and a lot of exercise and sport (30 – 60 min/day) are a healthy combination. The right weight furthers well-being and health. Thermals, directional effectiveness, digestive power

There are various criteria for judging the effectiveness of herbs and foodstuffs.

The use of certain herbs and ingredients is based on observations of the effects on the body which these foodstuffs, herbs and spices show after having eaten them. The medical science has developed following system: Every ingredient or herb has a directional effectiveness. Furthermore, there are herbs which have a special effect on certain organs.

The basic condition for a healthy metabolism is to obtain sufficient energy from food and that the digestive process doesn't use too much energy. An easily digestible meal makes content and sated, doesn't cause flatulence and fatigue after the meal. The perfect spices increase the healthiness of our meals. Very often, just small doses of herbs and spices will suffice. They are not used to make us sated, but to help our digestive organs to digest the food.

12.2 Recipes

The recipes list the ingredients to be used and the cooking instructions show how the dish is prepared. The list of ingredients shows the concerned quantities as well as the relevance for the therapy. If you find „less than mentioned", try to comply or find an alternative from the „list of recommended foodstuffs". Mostly it shall result just in a small change of taste when you simply avoid this ingredient.

Mild cooking methods: boiling, stewing, poaching, steaming
Strong cooking methods: barbecuing, roasting, frying, smoking
Balanced cooking methods: deep-frying, baking brick
Deep-freezing and warming in the microwave oven should be avoided (denaturalization).

12.3 Foodstuffs

Foodstuffs have an effect on body and soul like medicinal herbs, only a very much milder one. Dietary advice is mainly based on regional foodstuffs. The knowledge about the effects of each foodstuff and the knowledge, when which foodstuff shall be used, is based on the orthodoschool of medicine. Use ecologic-organic products, if possible. As everything should be cooked for a long time due to a better digestability and very rarely eaten raw, the food agrees with everyone.

The classification of the foodstuffs according to their effect on the body is the basis in order to achieve a harmonious status of health.

Dietary advisors do not recommend certain foodstuffs for everyone. The individual diet is tailor-made for the individual constitution.

Buy only fresh and ripe fruit and vegetables. You ought to leave unripe fruit and vegetables and such with brown spots and wilted leaves behind in the market. In this case take deep-frozen goods (never ready-to-serve dishes!). Fruit and vegetables are deep-frozen immediately after harvesting and often contain more vitamins and minerals than the goods from the vegetable shelf. Whereas conserved or tinned goods contain very much less biological substances. Also, salt, sugar and others are mostly added to the latter. Never leave the foodstuffs in the water after washing them to avoid that many vital substances get drowned. Clean salads, fruit and vegetables immediately before serving.

Please make sure of the hygienic processing of foodstuffs. Clean your salads, fruit and vegetables carefully. When cooking with meat, prepare all ingredients first and then process the meat products. Clean the worktop and tools very carefully. Wooden surfaces ought to be treated with a mild disinfectant regularly in order to reduce germination.

Store fruit and vegetables separately, if possible. Harvested fruit and vegetables are still alive and emit e.g. ethylene gas, which makes other products ripen and age faster. Keep meat and fish in the closed packaging or store them in the fridge in closed containers.

12.4 Herbs

There are some basic rules for storing medicinal herbs. On principle, herbs must be protected from direct sunlight, humidity and heat.

Containers for the storage of herbs may be glasses, ceramic jars and even plastic containers. However, plastic is a rather unsuitable material and should only be a short-term solution. In case of glass containers, use a dark material.

Medicinal herbs cannot be kept for any long period. The shelf life of herbs is limited. However, it can be prolonged with suitable storage. The place should be dark, rather cool and absolutely dry. A wooden medicine cabinet, placed not directly next to a source of heat, would be ideal. Never buy large quantities of herbs so as not to have to throw them away. Label the container with the name of the herb and the date of harvesting or processing.

13 Other dietic-books

The following syndromes of dietetics, TCM or for a therapy supplement for cancer are available.

Dietetics

E001. Nutrition of the infant - baby food
E002. Nutrition during lactation
E003. Nutrition in old age
E004. Nutrition of children and adolescents
E005. Nutrition of athletes
E006. Light weight
E007. Pregnancy
E008. Full food

Protein and electrolyte - kidneys
E009. (hemodialysis) dialysis treatment
E010. Acute renal failure
E011. Chronic renal insufficiency
E012. Nephrotic syndrome
E013. Kidney stones (nephrolithiasis)

Gastrointestinal tract - pancreas
E014. Acute pancreatitis (inflammation of the pancreas)
E015. Chronic pancreatitis (inflammation of the pancreas)

Gastrointestinal tract - small intestine and large intestine
E016. Acute obstipation (constipation)
E017. Chronic obstipation (constipation)
E018. Colon irritabile
E019. Diverticulitis
E020. Acquired lactose intolerance (lactose malabsorption)
E021. Fructose malabsorption
E022. Glutensensitive enteropathy (celiac disease)
E023. Colectomy
E024. Short Bowel Syndrome

Gastrointestinal tract - liver, gallbladder, bile ducts
E025. Acute and chronic hepatitis (inflammation of the liver)
E026. Cholelithiasis (bile stones)
E027. fatty liver
E028. cirrhosis

Gastrointestinal tract - Stomach and duodenal intestine
E029. Acute gastritis
E030. Chronic gastritis
E031. Stomach bleeding
E032. Ulcus ventriculi and duodenal ulcer
E033. Condition after gastric surgery

Gastrointestinal tract - oral cavity and esophagus
E034. Stomatitis
E035. Esophageal carcinoma (esophageal cancer)
E036. Refluosophagitis (heartburn)

Special diseases
E037. Phenylketonuria (PKU)
E038. Rheumatic joint diseases

Metabolism
E039. Obesity (overweight)
E040. Diabetes mellitus
E041. Eating disorders (underweight)

Fat metabolism
E042. Hypercholesterolaemia (increased cholesterol level)
E043. Hepatic Encephalopathy

Heart and circulation
E044. Arteriosclerosis (arterial calcification)
E045. Heart insufficiency
E046. Hypertension
E047. Hyperuricaemia and gout

Changed nutrient requirements
E048. In case of fever
E049. For malignant diseases
E050. After burns
E051. Radiation and chemotherapy

CANCER
E100. Pancreatic cancer
E101. Bladder cancer
E102. Blood cancer (leukemia)
E103. Breast cancer
E104. Colorectal cancer
E105. Gastric cancer
E106. Kidney cancer
E107. Esophageal cancer

TCM
E200. Bladder - moisture heat in the bladder
E201. Bladder - moisture and cold in the bladder
E202. Bladder - emptiness and cold In the bladder
E203. Large intestine - external cold affects the large intestine
E204. Large intestine - moisture heat in the large intestine
E205. Large intestine - heat blocks the intestine II acute
E206. Large intestine - dryness of the colon
E207. Large intestine - Yang deficiency (cold)
E208. Heart - Blood insufficiency
E209. Heart - Blood stagnation
E210. Heart - Fire
E211. Heart - Hot mucus clogs the heart pores

E212. Heart - Cold mucus clogs the heart pores
E213. Heart - Qi deficiency
E214. Heart - Yang deficiency
E215. Heart - Yin deficiency
E216. Liver - Ascending Liver Yang
E217. Liver - Blood deficiency
E218. Liver - Blood stagnation
E219. Liver - Moisture heat in liver and gall bladder
E220. Liver - Fire
E221. Liver - Gall bladder Qi-Empty
E222. Liver - Cold in the liver meridian
E223. Liver - Qi stagnation
E224. Liver - Wind
E225. Liver - Wind with ascending liver Yang
E226. Liver - Wind with blood anemic
E227. Liver - Wind with extreme heat
E228. Lung - Qi deficiency
E229. Lung - Mucus-moisture in the lungs
E230. Lung - Mucus-heat in the lungs
E231. Lung - Mucus-cold in the lungs
E232. Lung - Dryness of the lungs
E233. Lung - Wind-heat attacks the lungs
E234. Lung - Wind-cold affects the lungs
E235. Lung - Yin deficiency
E236. Stomach - Bloodstagnation
E237. Stomach - Fire
E238. Stomach - Cold with liquid
E239. Stomach - Nutrition stagnation
E240. Stomach - Qi deficiency
E241. Stomach - Rebellious Qi
E242. Stomach - Yin Emptiness
E243. Spleen - Heat and moisture attack the spleen
E244. Spleen - Coldness and moisture affects the spleen
E245. Spleen - Qi deficiency
E246. Spleen - Qi deficiency + Declining spleen Qi
E247. Spleen - Qi deficiency + spleen does not control the blood
E248. Spleen - Yang deficiency
E249. Kidney - Heart and kidney no longer communicate
E250. Kidney - Jing deficiency
E251. Kidney - Kidneys cannot receive the Qi
E252. Kidney - Qi is not stable
E253. Kidney - Yang deficiency
E254. Kidney - Yin deficiency

For further information visit di-book.com.